Stronger THAN PAIN

When years of continuous pain wracked
Arlene's body and plagued her mind,
would she find God's grace enough?

by
Arlene Kauffman
with Lori Yoder

Vision Publishers
Harrisonburg, VA

ISBN 10: 1-932676-17-1
ISBN 13: 978-932676-17-4

Many names and places have been changed to protect identity.

Edited by: Elizabeth B. Burkholder
Cover design and text design: Rhoda Miller

Printed in the United States of America

All Scripture taken from the King James Version unless otherwise indicated.

For information regarding special discounts for bulk purchases, please contact: Vision Publishers Orders at 1-877-488-0901 or write Vision Publishers at P.O. Box 190, Harrisonburg, VA 22803

Verses marked NIV are taken from the Holy Bible: New International Version, © 1978 by the New York International Bible Society. Used by permission of Zondervan Bible Publishers.

For information or comments write to:
Vision Publishers
P.O. Box 190
Harrisonburg, VA 22803
Fax: 540/437-1969
Phone: 877/488-0901
E-mail: orders@vision-publishers.com
www.vision-publishers.com
(see order form in back)

Preface

Through the years of physical pain and disability, I have prayed many times that God would use me in His service and that He would create in me a heart like Jesus'. But when another cloud of pain strikes, leaving me alone and in darkness, or when I sit looking at the signature line on yet another consent form I find myself asking, "God, where are You?"

"Child, I am here," He answers. "Where are you?"

Thousands of people enter hospitals for treatment, and leave with their problems solved. Coping with brief sickness or even death is one thing, but chronic pain can raise even bigger questions about God's goodness and wisdom. I struggle in coming to terms with the illness which not only debilitates me, but which also cripples the lifestyles of those who care for me. The thought of endless pain and continued dependence on others sometimes brings doubts and fears. But hope for improvement moves me to pick up the pen again, and sign the next consent form. I plead with the Lord to take the pain away, but He says to me:

> My grace is sufficient for you, for my power is made perfect in weakness. Therefore, I will boast all the more gladly about my weaknesses, so that Christ's power may rest on me. That is why, for Christ's sake, I delight in weaknesses, in insults, in hardships, in persecutions, in difficulties. For when I am weak, then I am strong (2 Corinthians 12:9, 10, NIV).

I don't understand this. A rabbi once said, "You have to get used to the paradox, because paradox is the only rationality large enough to handle the question."[1] God's ways confuse my mind, but I believe in my heart that the circumstances of my life are part of God's plan.

When people ask how I know it is God's will for me to suffer, I answer that my God makes no mistakes. He could intervene and heal me. He could lift me out of this body and give me the new one He has promised. To blame God would be foolishness. When I see beauty coming from ashes, joy rising out of mourning, and peace transcending my doubts, then I know it is my God who works the transformation. I have asked God to take my doubt and turn it into faith, to take the seeds of bitterness and turn them into blessing, to take my desert and turn it into an oasis for others. The deep peace I have felt even in the middle of intense pain amazes me. I stand as a witness to the Rock that is higher than I.

Many people have partnered with me on my journey through unusual physical illness, sharing my pain as they prayed, cared, and encouraged. Their continued interest in my story has provided impetus for this written record of God's faithfulness. I pray that you will enjoy God with me, for truly this is His story, and the ending is not yet written.

---

1 Conner, James A., *Silent Fire,* Crown Publishers: New York, 2002, p. 20.

Chapter 1

"Arlene, if you don't quit screaming, your mother will need to step outside."

The doctor peered at me beneath his bushy eyebrows. His face mask covered the lower half of his face and shrouded any comfort that a smile might have given.

"Van du net schtopsht greische dann muss ich naus geh" (*If you don't stop screaming, I have to go out of the room*), Mom told me. I was five years old and spoke only Pennsylvania Dutch.

The doctor worked to remove the cast that had protected my arm for six weeks. I had gone down to the cellar for a jar of tomato juice and tripped coming up the steps. The glass of the broken jar severed some tendons and sliced through a significant blood vein in my wrist. The blood gushing over my arm and the two hours I spent in the hospital the first time brought none of the terror I now felt, and the horrible noise convinced me he would cut into my arm while trying to remove my cast. None of my fears had come to pass when I escaped his office. "It will be okay," Mom said, and she was right. I have often whispered those words to myself since then, because God also has promised me, "It will be okay." And when I wake up in heaven some morning and see my Jesus Himself, I'll know He was right.

I turned six in August, shortly before school began. Since the law required that I attend school, I left my precious twin baby brothers and reluctantly went off to school. I was not the only first grader who knew only a smattering of English, but our teacher never showed her frustration at the formidable task of teaching her pupils English in addition to the regular lessons first graders must learn. I remember only her kindness.

The nightmares started when Miss Miller sent home information about the immunization shots required by the Garrett County Health Department. In my dreams at night, I bolted from the nurse. No matter how fast I ran, she always crept up behind me, her hands clutching needles and syringes, and I could hear myself screaming, frozen in terror-stricken slow motion as she grabbed me.

Nurse Mary Ellen was smiling and gentle, and she had only one syringe and one needle. "Wrap your arms around my waist in a big hug," she said. I closed my eyes and squeezed with all my might.

"Oooh, honey, not quite so tight!" she said. "Here it comes. It'll just be a little pinch." The pinch was a little one as promised; it certainly did not warrant the nighttime terrors I had suffered, but the nightmares had only begun. Within a few days, I came home from school with a fever of 103.7°. I cannot say with certainty that this is when my health problems began, for they did not all develop overnight. Before this, however, I seldom fought illness.

Childhood brought happy times for me. The good memories are especially precious, for the daddy I had in the early years slowly changed, and I now grieve that for most of my life I never really had a "daddy," mostly because he did not know how to express his love. We learned to work hard as youngsters, but we never thought of work as punishment; it needed to be done, and we did it. Mom also made certain that we had time to play, and many kittens suffered through hours of dress up and other little girl adventures. Life looked grand as we turned somersaults in crisp autumn leaves (until we tired of the apples falling on our heads) or tripped through the cow pasture to the woods, loaded with sandwiches, cookies, apples, lemonade, and kittens. Family excursions were fairly rare, but a day at the zoo gave us something to look forward to.

Jenny, a neighbor girl close in age to me and my sisters, often came over to play. If Mom had work that needed to be done, we kept busy and Jenny either joined us or sat and entertained us with her nonstop chatter. Jenny could send Martha and Miriam into giggles and shrieks until they heard Dad hollering from the shop, "Girls, cut it out!"

Wintertime brought splendid times of sledding when I was not in school. On the morning of the first good snow, we rushed through the breakfast dishes, hurriedly swept the floor, and bundled up for a fun time. When we did not have enough sleds for everyone, we used plastic bags and endured the soreness that followed.

Coming back into the house, famished and ready for lunch, we chattered excitedly to Mom about our tunnels and igloos and wild sled rides while the melting snow dripped into puddles at our feet. After we finally pulled off all our wet layers, Mom would send us for the mop. After the lunch dishes had been put away, we would decide it really had been such fun that we ought to go out again, so Mom would help us back into our sweaters and scarves, boots and mittens. My poor mother must have felt like sighing, but she never grumbled to us or made us feel guilty for our fun times.

One Sunday morning shortly before it was time to leave for church, Dad still had not started getting ready.

"Aren't you going to church today?" Mom asked. They had attended the Amish church in Oakland all their lives, and although she knew her withdrawn, resentful husband little resembled the Joe she had married, his decision came without any warning.

"No, I'm through with it."

"Where are you planning to go then?"

"Nowhere. I'll get the horse and buggy ready, and you can go."

Since Mom could hardly drive the horse and buggy and watch seven children, she left one of the twins, now two years old, at home with Dad. It was not long before Dad sold the horse and buggy and bought a van, but he did not mind if Mom attended church. Even though his bitterness against the Amish church must have been deep-seated, he continued to drive us to church and then picked us up after the service.

A man of few words, Dad never told us what really went on inside his heart or what turned him against his community, against his family, and against all he knew of God. We only saw his anger and unhappiness. Even Mom knew little of what fed his bitterness, but he informed her, "If these children turn out wrong, it'll be your fault." Our mother cried out to the Lord from the deepest part of her heart, telling Him she knew she could never raise her children alone.

We longed to feel Dad's love and approval, but his pent-up anger and terse ways often wounded our sensitive spirits. Even though he couldn't seem to show it, and even though he had built a thick wall between himself and other people, he really did love his children. I will never forget the times Dad spent helping me with my math homework; the times we spent together became special and are treasured in my heart.

"This looks like a good day to hike out and pick huckleberries in West Virginia," Dad announced one summer morning. After we were old enough to be of help, Dad took the family berry picking every summer.

"Oh, no!" we all groaned in unison, except for Alton, who against all reasonableness actually enjoyed picking huckleberries. Of all the cherries, sarves, blueberries, and huckleberries we picked, huckleberries were the worst. We packed a lunch and gathered up buckets and boots. The boots served as protective gear against rattlesnakes.

I thought we got there much too quickly, leaving too much time for fighting through the thick underbrush in search of berries. Dad made us a deal, promising to stop for ice cream cones for everyone who worked hard. David was not impressed about picking huckleberries, and no amount of ice cream could motivate him. "I don't care if I don't get ice cream," he declared after Mom tried her best to persuade him to change his mind. We had not been picking long before Alton appeared with a gallon bucket full of berries. For years, he had his own secret berry spots on the mountain and refused to let us follow him.

"Mom, how much longer will it be till we can go home?" I asked. "I'm so hot and tired."

"I don't know what Dad has in mind. He didn't tell me," Mom replied. "Are you not feeling good again today? What's wrong?" Mom asked.

"I'm just always so tired, and I feel funny." After a long, tiring day, our bowls and buckets were full and our mission was accomplished. I could hardly drag myself back to the van.

"Tasty Freeze ahead. What kind do you want?" Dad asked.

David just sat there while we licked our ice cream, and the fact that he did not get one took all the pleasure out of mine!

With his crew of seven energetic youngsters, Dad decided to start raising and selling garden produce. He plowed and harrowed a three-acre patch on top of the hill and set us to work. The rolling hills and the fertile fields of alfalfa, clover, and grass around us were deceptive. It would take aching backs, calloused hands, and hours of working out Adam's curse to turn this rocky patch into productive rows of beans, corn, tomatoes, and pumpkins.

After breakfast, I headed out to the produce patch with the rest of the family. Grasping a hoe, I set to work. After working for five minutes, leaving freshly turned earth behind me, I flopped down between the rows to rest, and then soon tried again. At fourteen years old, I had found my dream future: workaholic. I loved to work, and I thrilled to watch things happen under my hands. Like many childhood dreams, this one would never come true; I never lasted long before the hoeing and bending conquered me. Then I trudged back to the house to lie on the couch. I lay staring at the ceiling, waiting for the energy to get up to do the housework. God had already planned a special mission for me with a special label.

Chapter 2

Mom's concern grew as I complained about constant headaches, stomachaches, earaches, a racing heart, and fatigue. Because my stomach was queasy every time I ate and I had difficulty swallowing, I lost weight. Her mother's eye also noticed that my zest for life was waning. Disinterest and apathy were replacing my natural curiosity and spunk.

After yet another thorough examination by another doctor, we still had no answers. Dr. Nicol could give no explanation for my symptoms; he merely prescribed an antacid to soothe the burning in my stomach. During the two weeks before my next appointment, I lost four more pounds. I slept only when propped up with pillows so that I could breathe.

Two weeks came and went. There were more tests, more questions, and no answers. With the sinking disappointment, I also felt a strange hint of relief: perhaps no answer was better than a diagnosis condemning me to a slow and painful death or even to a tortured life.

After another two weeks, my pulse throbbed at 160, I was feverish, and I had lost three more pounds. This time the doctor, hoping he could locate any abnormalities, decided to call for an EGD, an abbreviation for *esophagogastroduodemscopy,* also called upper intestinal endoscopy. During this procedure, a flexible, imaging instrument (an endoscope) is passed through the mouth, into the esophagus, into the stomach, and then into the first portion of the small intestine, and duodenum.

Walking through the double doors in the hospital, I saw a big man being wheeled off the elevator. When I saw he had an IV attached to his arm, I felt pity for him, along with the relief that I had escaped those needles. When the nurse entered my room with a handful of needles, syringes, tubing and IV bags, my eyes widened and my jaw dropped. With a tremulous voice, I asked, "Are those for me?"

"Oh, yes, Hon. This will put you to sleep while we do the procedure," she answered, and then shook her head knowingly. "You don't want to be awake through this procedure." She then explained that they would not be able to sedate me too heavily until I had swallowed the endoscope. She assured me that I would remember little of the procedure. What should have been a relatively simple process became complicated when they experienced significant difficulty moving the tube through the esophagus. Despite their reassurances that I would be sedated, I soon found out that Arlene was the exception. I was alert when the endoscope reached my stomach, and I could hear the doctor talking about the excess bile he found. The bile in my stomach was eating the stomach lining like lye, so Dr. Nicol prescribed a powder that was supposed to absorb the excess bile.

Two weeks brought no improvement and I lost another four pounds. My legs seemed to have lost all their strength, and it took great effort to climb the long stairway to my bedroom and the bathroom. I crept up the stairs, hanging onto and pulling myself along the banisters. Dr. Daniel wanted to send me to a GI (gastrointestinal) doctor, one who specializes in the digestive tract.

"Matilda, this is getting serious, and I just don't know where to go from here," he told Mom. Both hospitals he mentioned were sixty miles from home, but I immediately chose Bear Creek Hospital. The second option had been the Western Maryland University Hospital, and I had the idea that university hospitals were for experimentation on patients who were beyond help. I knew my health situation was complex and was not looking hopeful, but I was definitely not ready to sign myself into that category.

Looking at other fifteen-year-old girls, I felt life was passing me by. The world and my friends moved on, laughing, working, looking toward the future. Other girls dashed up stairs, hoed and pulled weeds in the garden, and played softball with their friends. I needed to cling to the stairway banister, hauling myself up one step at a time. I lay in bed and wished my stomach would quit hurting. I checked my calendar for the next doctor's appointment. Why had God snatched me out of my active life? Why was He holding me suspended? Where was He?

Some people insinuated by their words and facial expressions that I was not as sick as I thought. I probably was using my illness as an excuse to lie on the couch instead of facing hard and unpleasant work. This confused and hurt me. Was I sick? Was I complaining and lazy? Could I make the sickness go away by thinking it away? While these questions haunted me, I knew deep inside that if I ever had the chance to work hard without pain, to run without nausea, I would never take it for granted.

Some compassionate people brought in a collection of surprises, a "sunshine box," to last three weeks. Although the rule was "one a day," I sometimes cheated and peeked when no one was close by to see and scold. I had little to think about other than my pain and what the doctors might find, so my mind settled on wondering what that box held until each little wrapped secret became a great mystery. Later, I got two more sunshine boxes and even some scrapbooks from communities where I knew no one. Never will I forget what caring like this meant. Never will I forget the love and warmth I felt when strangers took the time to show they cared.

After four months of doctor appointments and tests, no diagnosis had appeared. One day while Mom was sitting at the desk crying out to God in desperation, God gave her a thought: "Was Arlene's thyroid checked?" The following day, when I saw the doctor again, Mom asked him if he had checked my thyroid. Although he did not believe it to be the problem, he agreed to do the blood work. Two days later, our neighbor Irene came to the house with an urgent message from the doctor. "Tillie, you are wanted on the phone immediately over at our house."

I thought it was ridiculous that the doctor called to our neighbor's house. Surely I had the right to know first what was going on and what to expect. I was, after all, the one who was suffering.

"Mrs. Kauffman," Dr. Muir spoke tensely, "your daughter has a red hot thyroid and could go into a thyroid storm any minute. This could be fatal. Dr. Nicely is a thyroid specialist, and he'll be waiting to see her in the emergency room."

Although the seriousness of the situation should have frightened me, I felt excitement and joy: they had finally found the problem. Anything at all would be better than the interminable, impossible pain I felt and the shifting eyes and the helplessness that escaped from the doctors' professional, but empty, "we will take care of you" promises. Finally, I would have proof: the pain was real. I needed no psychiatrists or well-meaning churchgoers insinuating that it was all a mind game.

Chapter 3

I found Dr. Nicely waiting for me in the emergency room. He took one look at me and stopped short. "Are you Arlene?" He looked dubious.

"Yes." Of course I was Arlene.

He turned and looked at Mom. "I can't believe this! Most people with blood work numbers like hers are jittery and can't hold still for a minute. I can pick them out from across the street. But she . . . ." He looked at me again.

I was desperate. "But I do have headaches all the time, and earaches, and pressure behind my eyes, and I have trouble breathing and swallowing, and my stomach hurts, and . . . ." I needed an answer.

"Well, I can feel the thyroid is enlarged," he said a moment later, "and it is probably the source of undue pressure. As for your stomach problems, well, it is hard to make a diagnosis. You have too many things going on at the same time. Have patience with us until we get it ironed out." We were back to the vague platitudes. He continued, "Normally, we would be admitting a patient with results like hers, but I know you don't have insurance. I think I can let her go home, as relaxed as she is."

With an appointment for tests the next morning, and with clear warnings to come in the minute my symptoms escalated, he sent us home. We arrived home at one o'clock in the morning and were on the road again at six o'clock. Still, I felt hope.

Back in the doctor's office the next morning, Mom, Dad and I met with Dr. Muir and Dr. Nicely. The diagnosis was Graves' Disease, an autoimmune disease causing hyperthyroidism. The hyperthyroidism meant that my whole body functioned in high gear, working itself

 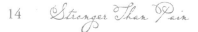

far too hard which was wearing down its own protective systems. Although severe Graves' Disease can be fatal when left untreated, treatment renders it nonthreatening. An X-ray showed clearly why I had difficulty swallowing and breathing when lying down, and Dr. Nicely sent me home with a prescription which was supposed to slow down my body's frantic hyperactivity.

For the first time in months, I actually improved. Maybe, just maybe, I could live a normal life after all. As the cloud of pain lifted, I found myself entering the world again, wondering what happened to whom, and where the neighbors were going, and why Dad was coming in from the barn already, and when the strawberries would ripen. I was becoming part of the present again, and it all mattered. The kittens in the barn mattered, and the bubbles on the rising bread mattered, and the bloom on the African violet on the windowsill mattered—all because I no longer needed to struggle to make my mind move beyond the pain that formed my own private world. Hope lasted for one wonderful week. Then my body reacted to the medication, and I developed a rash and a fever. Without the medication, I once again began the helpless downhill slide—losing weight and living in constant pain. After the brief, glorious reprieve, I had returned to the place where I would spend much of my life: the place of pain, of questioning, of waiting to find the way out.

When I visited the doctor in May, I went in a wheelchair because my sixteen-year-old legs no longer held my weight. Dr. Nicely, determined to get to the bottom of the problem, ordered complete bed rest. I had no idea then how long the pediatric wing at Bear Creek Hospital would be my home. The hospital was a world of shiny floors, stiff white uniforms, beepers, and alarms from intravenous pumps. Despite the sterile, controlled environment, interruptions were constant. Nurses were in and out at all hours of the night: nurses in squeaky shoes coming in for information, nurses flipping charts, nurses reading monitors, nurses asking me how I was doing when all I wanted was to sleep, painlessly, without interruption.

On my very first night in the hospital, they brought in a roommate just younger than me who had been in an accident following a drinking party. Just out of surgery, with one leg in traction and her head in a halo, she must have been a miserable and frightened girl. I lay in bed, too wide awake to sleep, when two policemen walked in to question her. When they found some drugs in her handbag, they mercilessly harangued the poor girl, and I trembled for her. I had grown up in a sheltered, rural home, and just the sight of the officers terrified me. My heart hurt for her, this girl my age who belonged to a world so strange to me. I longed to be able to do something for her, to touch her, and to show her a little of the peace and security I knew in spite of my health problems. I ached to show her Jesus, but we were so different, and I was so shy. What could I do? A nurse soon moved me to another room away from the disturbance, but I had glimpsed the world outside of what I had always known, and I felt a new determination to do all I could do from my hospital bed.

I was still losing a pound every two days because of my uncontrolled thyroid. It took almost too much energy just to bring food to my mouth and to chew, and breathing was still difficult. I could not stand on the scales, so they used a surfboard and hoisted me up.

Unpleasant and long as this hospital stay felt, I learned to love the staff and made many friends. They often dropped by with candy bars or other treats, and they seemed to like me. After I mentioned to one nurse that I liked baking, she said, "Let's make a deal: once you get back on your feet, you go home and bake us a bushel of cinnamon rolls with lots of caramel icing."

"Yeah, I'd like to do that. You've been so good to me." I smiled groggily. "But do you know how much a bushel would be?" I asked, even while plans rolled around in my weary mind.

One day, a physician's assistant, Dr. Frank Pinto, was on duty and stopped in to examine me because of my shortness of breath. A few days later, he stuck his head around the curtain again just to say "hi." He pulled up a chair beside my bed, took my hand, and sat down to chat. "Is there something I can do for you? You aren't necessarily my patient, but I'll be in and out checking on you. Maybe I can be a middleman for you and interpret all that medical terminology." His eyes twinkled. "You are a favorite around here I hear." He wanted to know how I was doing, not because he had a chart to fill out, but because he cared. His warm smile and his genuine attention to how I was feeling instantly set him apart. From that day on, he was "Frank."

The hospital personnel often commented about all my friends, and the walls around my bed were filled with cards. Some of those cards were from people I didn't know, and the care I felt from strangers touched me and surrounded me with arms of love, like a hug from God. I knew I would never forget that feeling. "If I ever get better," I promised myself, "I will reach out to those who hurt. I'll be a blessing whether I know them or not."

After I had a spell during which my heart raced and I could hardly breathe, I was moved across from the nurses' desk so they could keep a close eye on me. It had been six weeks, and still I could not hold my own weight.

Again Frank came in and pulled up a chair by my bedside expressing his concern. "Arlene, you aren't improving. According to your blood work, you're on the verge of a thyroid storm. What would you think about going to Grant Town to the university hospital?"

"If they can make me feel better, I'll go." No, I didn't want to go, but I too was getting desperate.

"Dr. Nicely has been talking with Dr. Peck in Grant Town because they're up to date with the research and equipment. We've been ready for the transfer weeks ago, but Dr. Muir wanted to do all he could first. I think it's past time to move on. If you're okay with it, I'll talk to him again." Frank could hardly bear watching me waste away while Dr. Muir "did all he could." I had lost seventy pounds in six months, and Frank was worried.

The arrangements were soon made for the move to Grant Town, and Frank and the nurses in the pediatric wing did their best to prepare me for the changes I could expect in a university hospital.

"Good morning, Arlene!" Frank stepped in with his usual smile.

"How are you feeling about the move? You're such a quiet girl. If you have any questions, you can ask us, you know."

I was apprehensive about all the changes that would come with the transfer, so I asked questions about what to expect. Since they train thousands of doctors and nurses in the university hospital, Frank warned me that doctors and students would be in and out of my room often, asking the same questions over and over again. I still dreaded feeling like an experiment in Grant Town, but I knew in my heart that my heavenly Father knew how I felt, and I really did want His will.

One day Mom asked me whether I remembered that my dear friend Saloma was getting married in Virginia that weekend. My condition was so serious that some people in our extended family wondered if perhaps they would need to choose between attending a wedding or a funeral. I never could have guessed then what an important part Saloma would continue to play in my life.

While I lay in bed thinking about the transfer to another hospital, life back home never slowed down. The produce patch on the farm kept everybody busy, and Dad was depending on the produce to help pay for the rapidly accumulating medical expenses. Although the bills appeared insurmountable, Dad never accused me of not being worth the money and time. He did, however, complain of the doctors not being worth their time and money. Dad never paid some of the bills. His philosophy was that if the hospitals were of no help, they did not deserve the money. He received nasty letters from authorities and collecting agencies for those outstanding bills, but nothing ever came of their threats.

One day, Dad put a recliner bed in the back of the van for the ninety-mile ride to Grant Town. With many goodbyes from the staff, and with some candy bars tucked into my bag, I got settled in the makeshift bed and headed to Grant Town. When we arrived, they paged Dr. Peck who soon arrived.

"Hi, I'm Dr. Peck. I understand you are having some rough times with your thyroid. A young girl your age shouldn't have all these problems," he said. "Your abdominal problem has everybody stumped, too. Tell me about it. When did it start?"

The questions had begun. "I've had abdominal pain for years," I answered. "As time goes on, it just gets worse and worse, and it's harder to swallow too."

"Your thyroid is running in high gear. That is why any action on your part causes your heart to race, making you short of breath. I would like to run some more tests and try a couple drug combinations to see what we can do for you," Dr. Peck explained.

From there, I was taken to a ward on the eighth floor. I had not been in my room long before Dr. Ruby, a resident doctor who worked with Dr. Peck, stopped in with a barrage of questions and a prediction that he would be back in the morning with eight to ten students. Late that night, two students repeated the same old questions. Impatient and exhausted with the stress of facing all the new people, I wondered why they did not just read my charts. Still uncomfortable around strangers, I spent a sleepless night. At six o'clock, Dr. Ruby entered with his passel of students with clipboards and their inquiries. This was Grant Town.

The three older ladies in my ward provided quite a switch from the pediatric ward to which I'd grown accustomed. Doctors, students, baths, sheet changes, medications, and blood work added together and multiplied by four yielded little peace and quiet, but we quickly developed a camaraderie.

"Well, if it isn't Arlene's friend, Dr. Ruby, coming in to see her again. Isn't he cute? I think he likes to come see Arlene," Rose chirped. Rosie, as we called her, was a charming elderly lady with a delightful presence that kept our ward sounding merry even though we each had our own pack of troubles. Rosie carried with her a twenty-four hour heart monitor that regulated her heart's functioning, and she was required to carefully document all her activities on a chart.

"Girls, I am going to take a walk down the hallway," she said one morning, "and I guess I better write down what time I'm getting out of bed." A while later, we heard her chuckling as she came down the hallway and back into the room.

"What is it, Rosie?" we asked her.

"I dropped my paper on the floor," she said, laughing, "and then I had to record that I bent down to pick it up, and now I better document all my giggling." Rosie had a way of helping us forget where we were. "You know what, gals?" she said. "You won't believe this, but I think this is the first time I have laughed since my husband passed away a year ago." We found that healing happens in more ways than one, and the Proverb proved true: "A merry heart doeth good like a medicine" (Proverbs 17:22).

On another day, I found myself in need of the healing that comes to the heart, and just when I needed it, God sent a stack of cards from various people. That day I believed, and I still do, that angels are often disguised as friends. In that pile of cards was one from my friend Frank from Bear Creek Hospital. It had this message:

1. Why do doctors wear masks?
   You will understand when you get your bill.
2. Should you let the doctor put one of those sticks in your mouth?
   Not until you know who ate the ice cream.
3. Why does the hospital serve so much chicken soup?
   Because the chickens won't eat it.
4. Does the hospital serve blended coffee?
   Yes, they blend yesterday's with today's.
5. Why should I avoid pressing the buzzer button?
   It wakes the nurse.
6. May I remove this plastic name band on my wrist?
   No, you're wearing little enough as it is.

Two or three days later, the candy striper came with a card signed by forty people from various departments at Bear Creek Hospital. That card and others like it proved invaluable in making me feel loved and important even though I often felt like a burden to others as my hospital stay dragged on.

Rosie came bursting in the door from her jaunt down the hall, puffing and looking wildly behind her as though her nightmare monsters had materialized and were breathing down her neck. She slammed the door shut. Then, not giving her all-important clipboard and now hardworking heart a thought, the little woman hauled a large recliner against the door and piled it with visitors' chairs and everything else of substance that she could find to use as a blockade.

"What happened?" we asked, our eyes wide and our hearts pounding. We had seen a passel of doctors and nurses running down the hall minutes before, but we couldn't imagine what danger might be turned loose on our floor.

Between her gasps for breath, Rosie managed to say, "A . . . a big . . . a big man . . . from the psychiatric unit . . . he was going into people's rooms!"

Eventually, after we finally decided it was safe to remove our blockade, the nurse stopped in to check on one of the women in our ward. We asked what had happened. The nurse told us that the patient had left our wing and had run into another patient's room, where he grabbed the bedpan and chucked it at the window. He'd just been ready to jump when a doctor caught him.

Later that week, live drama once again came to our floor. This time, we heard a great commotion coming from across the hall. When Rosie asked a nurse what was going on, the nurse told us that the female staff members were no match for the uncooperative male patient. The banging and hubbub we heard came as our neighbor fought the restraints they'd needed to put on him. "Once I let him loose so he could feed himself," the nurse told us, "and I was standing right there, but just that quick, whoosh went his food tray. The food was all over me and the wall, the whole way up to the ceiling."

We gasped and looked at each other. What kind of neighbor did we have? She continued, "Another time he slipped his restraints and locked himself in the bathroom. He turned on the faucet, and when we heard the noise and went to his room, we saw water running out from under the bathroom door. He wouldn't unlock the door, so we called maintenance. They took the door off the hinge for us." She shook her head. "You never know what might happen—keeps life interesting." She left to go see her next patient, and as I lay in bed, I wondered how safe I actually was here in this hospital.

But the following weeks held little such excitement, and the hours stretched into days, long and lonesome. Roommates share this journey in ways healthy people cannot, and Mary Robinette was one who provided our ward with incessant chatter. After she went home, the chatter continued in six to eight page letters, coming to me two or three times a week. Both sides of the lined notebook pages were full. I kept in contact with Mary until the cancer ended her life.

After years of hospital stays and hundreds of roommates, however, I know Rose still holds a place in my heart no one else can replace. She left a vacancy much bigger than an empty bed when eventually she was released from the hospital, even though her daughter came to see me two or three times a week as long as I was in Grant Town.

July 21, 1981 became another mile marker for me. Mom and Dad had come to the hospital to visit when Dr. Peck unexpectedly asked to meet with us. "We have Arlene on the last drug we can use to treat Graves' disease," he began, "and we've seen little improvement. There's just nothing more we can do at this point besides surgery, and that's not an option because of the condition of her thyroid."

This was no news. Where was he going with this conversation?

"She seems to be pretty stable," he continued, "so how would you feel about taking her home?"

"Today?" was all I could say.

"Yes, today," he said. "We're always here if you need something." He looked at Mom and Dad. "I'll give you a few minutes to talk it over and I'll be back."

Home. Home? Home! It was the first time in nine weeks I had heard the beautiful word. I longed to go home, yet I had thought they would fix all my problems, then send me home. I still spent most of my time in bed. Every time I tried to walk, my legs collapsed and my heart rate skyrocketed. Were they writing me off as a hopeless case? We dubiously agreed to give it a try.

Dad quickly drove home to rent a hospital bed and wheelchair. He then gave my excited sisters instructions for preparing the sewing room for its conversion into an invalid-friendly ward. The whole family cheered when we finally arrived home, and Dad carried me into the house that suddenly seemed strange and unfamiliar. I felt both elation and hesitation. Although I was completely weary of hospital food and hospital smells and hospital schedules, I knew I still was not well. I also knew that my family would continue to make many sacrifices because of my illness. I could do almost nothing for myself, and in spite of their genuine love and care, I never could quite feel that my life was anything but a burden.

Chapter 4

After three weeks at home, I clearly was going downhill again. My heart rate was much too high, swallowing was all but impossible, and if the food did reach my stomach, it brought on nausea and pain. When Mom decided to call Dr. Peck, I was ready for a change, any change.

Dr. Peck's response was resigned. "This is what I expected. Bring her in."

Because of my poorly functioning immune system, surgery brought significant risk. The medical team, hoping to prepare my body for surgery, decided to insert a tube through my nose into my stomach, bypassing the enlarged thyroid and allowing them to "feed" me antibiotics. Although the doctor tried to be gentle, those who have never experienced the procedure can only imagine the discomfort. If people still questioned the validity of my health complaints or wondered if perhaps I was just trying to get attention, they hopefully laid aside all doubts. Nobody could possibly want this sort of attention.

Days turned into weeks, and still my doctors set no date for surgery. Dad reached his limit of patience. He marched out to the front desk, insisted on talking to the doctor, and demanded a surgery date. "Three weeks is long enough! Every day in the hospital is costing big money we just don't have." My thyroidectomy was scheduled for September 24, 1981.

The evening before surgery when Dr. Otto, chief surgeon, came to explain the procedures and risks involved, I quickly understood why this huge man had been dubbed the "Big Bear." While I dreaded surgery, the risk it involved affected my family more than it did me. I had worried little about not surviving surgery, but the surgeon's warning that the procedure could damage my voice troubled me. What if I could never speak again? Could I live with a handicap like that?

At nine o'clock that night, a "cleaning crew" came by with a wheelchair to take me to the whirlpool bath. They used Betadine solution and a scrub brush to give me a merciless scrubbing to prepare me for surgery in the morning. They knew my body could not handle infection, and when they finished, I knew I had never been so clean in my life!

When Mom walked in the next morning before surgery, she was alone. "Where is Dad?" I asked.

"He drove me down, then went back home to fill silo," she said, and then added apologetically, "You know how he hates hospitals."

My surgery was scheduled for seven o'clock, and the nurses informed Mom that she could expect me to be coming into the recovery room at one o'clock that afternoon. Mom sat alone in the waiting room, watching the hours slowly pass and wondering if her daughter would live through this ordeal.

"Well, Mrs. Kauffman, we got into more complications than we expected, but everything went well. Arlene's thyroid was two and a half times its normal size, and instead of showing up outside like it often does in cases like this, it crowded against the windpipe. It certainly explains why she had trouble swallowing and breathing." He had also needed to cut some strap muscles in my neck. As soon as she heard that my condition appeared to be stable, Mom called home to pass on the good news to my anxious family and the many friends who had been praying for me.

When I woke up from my first surgery, my helplessness frightened me. I could not feel my arms, I could not move my head, I could not wipe my tears.

The doctor spoke, "Arlene, can you hear me? Tell me your name."

I mustered all my strength and whispered, "I . . . I . . . ." I was terrified! Would I ever speak again? Would I be reduced to whispering all my life? But the doctor turned to Mom and said, "She'll be okay."

Mom stood beside me and spoke in a soft voice. "Arlene, I just praise God for the way you're lying here peacefully, and you're breathing normally. He saved your life, daughter."

One week after surgery, I was still unable to lift my arms or even hold my head, but the physical therapist came in, loaded me into a wheelchair, and started wheeling me down the hall. We met Dr. Peck, who stopped the therapist and demanded, "Where are you taking her?"

"Physical therapy," the therapist answered.

"Oh no, you aren't. You turn around and take her right back upstairs to her bed," the doctor snapped.

A few minutes later, he barged into my room, obviously upset. He turned to Mom and exploded, "She's nowhere near ready for physical therapy! It's going to take time to get her to where she can handle a workout. She's been a very sick girl for months already, and her body just went through a major trauma."

After he left, I lay there and wondered if I would ever fully recover. Maybe I would never live a normal life. Could I handle that?

Many of these days were dark, and small irritations, like the man across the hall who hiccuped for two days straight, brought me to a place of desperation. Questions and doubts about my future often weighed heavily on my mind. Time after time, I found myself turning to the only One to whom I knew to turn. The Lord Jesus always provided the strength to live that day, and the next, and the next.

A few bright rays of light pierced through these shadowed days, like the surprise box from the staff at Bear Creek Hospital. I still lacked the strength to hold my head on my own, but I watched eagerly as Mom pulled out what I thought must be the loveliest, fuzziest, blue housecoat and then grabbed at the candy bars that fell out of its folds.

I was finally released from the hospital five weeks later, once again able to swallow and breathe properly, but I was still suffering from undiagnosed stomach problems. After eight months of living in beds and wheelchairs, the hard hours of physical therapy paid off, and I took my first solo steps on Christmas Eve. I thought it was the perfect Christmas gift!

When Dr. Peck saw me for my follow-up appointment in January, he came in, then stopped with a puzzled look on his face. "Where's your wheelchair?"

"Out in the waiting room!" I replied proudly.

"Arlene, I can't believe this! You can get out of your chair by yourself? I need to see this." All my hard work combined with my family's faithful, tender loving care was paying off.

"Hey," he said, "if I give you my arm, can you make it to the conference room? They need to see you!" He took my arm, and I faltered down the hallway. "Do you know who this is, folks?" The doctors in the conference room had to look twice before they believed their eyes, and even the nurses did not recognize me immediately. I had not gone far before my legs trembled and sweat appeared on my forehead, but that day they all felt they were seeing a walking miracle.

Seven years before, when I was ten and my brother James was twelve years old, he was diagnosed with diabetes. Because of his extremely high sugar levels, he had been admitted to the hospital to be examined by a pediatric doctor. This terrified me, for somewhere I had gotten the idea into my childish mind that if someone was sick enough to be admitted to the hospital, it meant that person would surely die.

I definitely challenged my own stereotypes many times and have shocked others as well. I might have despaired and given up many times, but even while I was quite young, Mom often had noted her eldest daughter's independent personality. I did not require any help from my parents or my two older brothers, thank you very much. This spirit and spunk probably got me over some hurdles later in life that might have daunted anyone less thick-headed.

I came by my stubbornness honestly. Dad was a strong, driven man, often running and whistling as he worked. He sometimes worked too hard, and on the day I was born, Dad took Mom to the hospital and then returned home because three of his brothers had come to help him build a new dairy barn. When he called the hospital to see if Mom was doing okay, the nurse told him he had a baby girl! Self-sufficient and determined to pay off his debt load, he worked with a carpenter crew during the week and still managed to keep a small dairy herd by farming before and after work and on Saturdays.

Mom also had her share of that special grit that borders on foolishness. After the birth of the twins, Danny and David, the doctor started showing concern for her and asked, "Matilda, you haven't been up much, and the babies are several days old now. What seems to be the problem?" Mom, determined to get home to her husband and five older children, excused herself as best she could without letting him know how terribly her back hurt when she walked or sat. We had just moved into a new house, and she had five children waiting at home. Alton, the oldest, was not yet ten. Four days later, Mom tried to persuade the doctor to release her, telling him how she felt needed at home, but he wisely replied, "You're better off where you are for a few more days. We will talk then about going home."

After crying her heart out and talking to God about all her worries, Mom tried to relax for the sake of her babies. For years, however, she worked in spite of severe back pain. I would later see how the strength and determination I had inherited from my parents would prove to be important in my life.

One day that spring, Dad planned to go to Accident and wondered if I still wanted to take cinnamon rolls to the staff at Bear Creek Hospital. I knew I couldn't do the baking alone, but with Mom's help, I soon had freshly baked rolls with caramel frosting ready to go. I thought they would be delighted with the rolls, but the nurses at the front desk looked startled. I heard some nurses down the hall asking, "Is that Arlene?" They came with big hugs as soon as they were convinced it really was the Arlene they knew. Someone called Frank, the laboratory and X-ray technicians, and the staff from the physical therapy, dietary, and housekeeping departments. The many people I had come to know during those six long weeks created quite a crowd.

Frank had just come in when he was paged. As he went out the door, he said, "I'm sorry, Arlene. Don't leave before I get back because I have something I want to talk to you about."

Before he got back and before I was ready to leave, Mom came in saying, "Dad's in a hurry. You need to come right away."

I was miserable. I thought I simply could not leave the hospital before Frank returned, but I had little choice. Dad could be the most friendly, congenial man one minute and become a frightening, angry person the next minute, particularly if an apparently innocent conversation with a friendly visitor turned out to be an attempt to convince him of his guilt and need for God. He truly loved us children, but because it did not take much to trigger his rage, we learned at a young age to avoid angering him.

Only a few weeks later, I received a phone call from Bear Creek Hospital: "Arlene, we're calling to let you know that Frank was killed in a car accident yesterday." The news broke my heart. Frank had stayed with me through so many rough times, and he had been so much more than a physician's assistant; he had been a friend. I often wondered what it was that he wanted to say.

Chapter 5

The summer I was sixteen years old, Dad bought a farm in Bittinger, Maryland, named the "Nayburlee Farm" in honor of the community people who had rebuilt the barn after it was destroyed by fire. When Dad first took his family to the farm for a workday, I formed a strong opinion before I had even stepped out of the van. The house looked like a dungeon, the buildings were rundown, the lawn was a hayfield, and the whole farm was a community junkyard.

A quick tour cemented my opinion. Old clothes, toys, and other pieces of junk were strewn through the decrepit buildings and in the ditches. My brothers called, "Hey, girls, come here!" We ran to the barn to see what new horrors it held and found three dead cows and a foot of manure!

The ramshackle house with dark green shingles was little better, reeking of dogs and cats that had inhabited it. Dad, hoping to build a new house eventually, did not want to invest much money in repairing the old one although its buckling, hundred-year-old foundation and seventeen cracked or broken windows made it a sorry sight. But it did have seven good windows! The kitchen linoleum was completely worn through, and the basement held an antique barber's chair cemented into the floor as well as sodden coal ash eight inches thick. My strength was very slow in returning since my surgery, and the idea of moving into this disaster zone overwhelmed me. Some friends and relatives came to help, bringing buckets, brushes, strong soaps, and lots of energy. After one long day, the house was still no mansion, but it was clean.

As I think of all that Mom must have dealt with during this time,

I once again wonder at the strength God gave her. She was entering a new community, one in which family and church were of utmost importance, as she was without a husband's support. Dad had not attended the Amish Church with us for twelve years now, and Mom decided to begin attending Mountain View Mennonite Church, eighteen miles north of Bittinger. We all hoped and prayed that Dad would choose to make a new start, but he showed no interest in making any life changes, so Mom made this decision alone. We children decided to join her.

Moving into a new community meant that we were leaving our friends and cousins thirty miles away in Oakland. Our social interactions were now based entirely around church on Sunday, since the Amish church seldom encourages education beyond eighth grade. We had just left the Amish church, and until James got his driver's license, none of us could legally drive.

My sisters and I often felt lonely and isolated on our small farm, but we found a camaraderie between us because of all the experiences we shared. Mom also knew how much we children needed friends, and I know her heart hurt for us. We sometimes invited guests for Sunday lunch, but visitors often seemed a bit nervous, wondering if they were totally welcome and hoping Dad did not object to their presence. Truthfully, we too were nervous, hoping he would not yell at Mom, hoping he would not embarrass us, hoping that we could make it a pleasant time for our guests. Dad sometimes sat in the living room with us although he rarely contributed to the conversation, only tersely answering any questions. I often wondered, in times like these, what was happening inside his heart. I thought how lonely and cold it must feel, and I felt sadness for my father.

Dad often did the grocery shopping. Sometimes he came home with the items on Mom's grocery list, and sometimes he figured we could do without, but Dad always made certain we had all the sugar we needed. He loved his sweets, and entering the Christmas season, we never needed to wonder what treats Dad expected even though he rarely spoke much. Fruitcakes, coconut bonbons, peppermint patties, chocolatey Rice Krispy candy, chocolate-covered cherries, and peanut butter balls were all part of the season's traditions. Although Mom's schedule never left spare minutes, making Dad's favorites became a way she always showed her love for him. Dad and my brothers were avid hunters, and the opening of deer season was one event that kept them out of the house for most of the day, allowing Mom and us girls to fill containers with homemade candy. Of course, we had to hide the goodies; if we had not, they would never have lasted until Christmas Eve!

The summer we moved to Bittinger, I asked to be baptized and became a member of Mountain View Mennonite Church. In a new and meaningful way, I was telling the world that I had given my life to the mastery of Jesus Christ. I had grown up hearing about God's plan for me, how He had let His own Son die so that I would not need to die for all the wrong I had done. In the years that followed, this picture of a God who suffered took on whole new levels of meaning for me. Here was someone who knew what pain felt like. He was a man of sorrows and acquainted with grief. He also taught me, slowly and patiently, what it meant to live as His child.

The time I spent that winter working in Jerry and Ruth's home became a special part of this learning process. Ruth was expecting a new baby, and with two active youngsters and a house to care for, she was not able to care for herself as well as she needed to. I knew Jerry and Ruth Yoder only as acquaintances from church, but it did not take long for me to see that I would love them and their children, Lori and Nathan, whose energy made me wish for a fraction of what they had. Since the job involved housework instead of garden and lawn care, it was perfectly suited to my needs.

Ruth was a sweet, friendly lady who did all she could to make my work enjoyable, and their home opened my eyes to what a Christian home could be. Of course, we all had grumpy days, but the atmosphere was one that exuded peace and happiness instead of the tension we so often felt at home in spite of Mom's efforts to maintain peace. The lifestyle here was completely different, too. Though Jerry got up early to milk cows, the family sat down for a family worship time before breakfast. Before leaving for church on Sunday morning, Jerry gathered his family around him as he knelt to ask God to be with both the pastors and with the members who would meet together at church. Clearly, he cared deeply for his family and took his role as a father seriously. Less than a year later, he was ordained as a leader in the church.

By the time the baby arrived and Ruth was feeling well, the freezer was stocked with cookies, cinnamon rolls, and bread. We even made doughnuts one day, to the delight of Lori and Nathan, who loved "helping." I still cherish the time I spent in their home as a special gift from God.

During my later teen years, I also took some jobs caring for the elderly in their homes. Because of my health problems, I knew I could not handle the stress that would come with most strictly scheduled jobs, so there were few options open to me.

Like any other teenage girl, I wondered what my future held, but instead of my first questions being *what* I would do or *where* I would go or *with whom* I would spend my life, I wondered whether I would be healthy enough to enjoy my life. Would I ever have a home like I had seen at Jerry and Ruth's? Would I ever be strong enough to own and run my dream bakeshop? Could I avoid hospitals for the rest of my life? Like every other girl, I lived one day at a time.

Chapter 6

Cinty was an elderly lady undergoing cancer treatments, and her stepdaughter hired me to cook, to do some light housework, and to be a companion to Cinty. The tiny house in Springs, Pennsylvania, had no bathtub or shower and only one commode which was located in the basement. I understood that changing this might be a bit of an investment and would likely have meant adding onto the house, but the clutter collection, I thought, was entirely unnecessary. The boxes were stacked high in my room, leaving only enough room for me to turn around. They were full of scraps from a shirt factory. Old magazines filled the boxes surrounding the living room. Cinty's collecting days were not yet over, for each week she sent me to the local bulk food store for whatever items happened to be on sale. I had orders to buy whatever it was, just because it was on sale. To my chagrin and secret amazement, she always managed to find a place to put the random groceries I carried home.

I wanted to please the lady whose cancer treatments clearly left her feeling unwell, but some days the task seemed impossible—she found fault with all I did until every trip I made out of the house for mail or groceries felt like an escape from Cinty's scrutiny. That winter the coal furnace was a particular trial, and we suffered through the alternating heat and cold as I learned how to regulate the temperature. Cinty growled, her stepdaughter teased, and I sweated.

Although the agreement with my employer allowed me plenty of time for myself and any hobbies I chose to bring along, I think it may have been a mistake for me to pull out a sewing machine. I worked hard but happily those first days, and before I knew it, I had cut and pieced two log cabin quilt tops for Mom. The damage was done, and Cinty now had big plans for me. She delved into those exasperating boxes stored in my bedroom and triumphantly supplied enough scraps for more quilts than I ever hoped to quilt. After I finished piecing one for her, she uncovered a set of quilting frames she had stashed away somewhere. I had no idea how we could set up a frame for a quilt the size of a double bed in this tiny living room, but we managed. I had to crawl underneath the quilt to get into my bedroom or into the kitchen, so I got busy, knowing the faster I worked the sooner I would have my walking space back.

I cut, pieced, and quilted that first quilt in twelve days. In Cinty's mind, it was only proper for a young person to wake early and work hard all day, so even when visitors came, I heard her sharp voice: "You can quilt while you talk, Arlene." Cinty's stepdaughter could see my "boss" was driving me too hard and spoke to her about it. But Cinty kept her high expectations, and I just wanted to avoid her remonstrations at all cost. If I turned each quilt into a race against my own record, it became a bearable challenge. I pieced and quilted nine quilts for Cinty during the nine months I spent with her. She gave some away, but most she sold.

I do admit to a few small tricks of self protection during my time working there. Cinty planned all the menus, and one day she sent me to the basement for some meat from the freezer. When I opened the freezer, my face blanched and I slammed it shut, then sneaked another look. Right there on top lay a groundhog. I quickly tucked it into the bottom of the freezer and stacked other food on top to hide the critter. I certainly did not want groundhog appearing on the menu!

My second act of subterfuge also concerned vermin. Just as I dozed off in the darkness one night, I felt something warm and fuzzy move at my neck. Too terrified to move at first, I then sat bolt upright, and a mouse shot out across the bed. For my peace of mind, I thoroughly searched the bed. Although my investigation produced no nest of mice, all those boxes of fabric now looked alarming. I knew what Cinty would say if I asked for a mousetrap. "You must be leaving the basement door open. How else could they get into the house? Why can't you just close the door?" I wanted to avoid that censorious voice at all costs, so I quietly crept through the dark house and borrowed a mousetrap from our next door neighbors who had not yet gone to bed. I slipped back into my bedroom and set the trap, but sleep was far away while my imagination worked overtime in the vermin department. Soon, the trap snapped. I disposed of the contents and set it again. Again it snapped. I caught five mice that night.

After Cinty passed away, I accepted another position and went to stay with Roy and Clara. Their daughter Brenda met me at the door in the lower level of their house the first time I went to visit. With tears in her eyes, Brenda described the personality changes she had seen, particularly in her mother, as Clara aged and her once refined sensibilities changed. "We had a serious talk with them before contacting you," Brenda said. "I know they can be difficult sometimes, and if they refuse to cooperate, they'll be on their own again. They get so lonely when the only person coming in is the cleaning lady."

We paused before going upstairs, and we heard Clara's voice instructing her husband, "Now you better behave yourself or the little girl won't stay."

That first week, both of my charges were good as gold. Roy, always wearing brown corduroy pants and plaid shirts, spent hours in his rocking chair by the window, reading the newspaper or listening to the books on tape that the Oakland Public Library sent out for him. Clara sat upright in her chair beside him, twisting her handkerchief, her daintily printed dresses meticulously pressed, and her white hair matching the lace at her throat. Her eyes followed me solemnly everywhere I went, but in those first days she said hardly a word, apparently afraid that "the little girl" would leave. As she became accustomed to "the little girl" in their house, her unnaturally quiet personality disappeared. The minute I walked out of her sight, she would let loose a string of expletives, calling me every name in the book.

"Little girl, it is dinner time. What are we going to have? I am hungry," became a regular refrain. Then at mealtime, she would move to the next stanza of her song: "Little girl, this tastes awful and I don't want to get fat," she would say as she often dished out a large helping, followed by a second and sometimes a third.

She made slow, regular rounds through the house, and every fifteen minutes I would see Clara appear at the door with her walker to investigate my doings. She then took her reports back to Roy who wearied of her worries and continuous commentaries. The two constantly bickered back and forth. It often began with Clara. "The little girl is going to church; is she going to come back?" Then she would follow up with the usual, "You better be good."

"Can't you just sit down and be quiet?" he would often reply and then add in all sincerity, "If you don't settle down, I'll divorce you yet, even if you are ninety."

Clara was a poor sleeper and called for me two or three times during the night. "Little girl, is Roy sleeping? What were you doing? What time is it?"

Although I was given a lovely place to stay and had plenty of time and space for my own hobbies, the days became monotonous for me, and my charges often seemed like cantankerous children who tried my patience. I was eighteen years old and still young enough to hope that life could give me more. Over and over again, I reminded myself how lonely they were, how Jesus showed compassion to those around Him, and how I could make their lives more pleasant.

Clara became wearisome, but it was Roy who eventually was nearly impossible to deal with. He started sneaking up behind me, giving me a big smooch on my cheek before I even knew he was close by. It did not take long before I learned to keep my ears open for the sound of his shuffling feet coming toward me so that I could quickly head in the opposite direction. Next he started begging for a kiss.

"No way! I am not handing out kisses!" I told him emphatically.

"I'll give you ten dollars for each kiss!" Roy offered. When I told him in no uncertain terms that I would not consider it, he showed surprise. "You'll pass on ten dollars just for a kiss?" he asked.

"I sure will!" I replied. Roy certainly had more money than sense, I decided. Then once in the middle of the night, I was startled out of a deep sleep. "Roy, what are you doing in here?" I yanked the bedding back and was up and out of bed like a bullet as he came and crawled into it! I slipped out into the living room and crouched behind the recliner, thinking this seemed like some crazy dream. I was suddenly ever so thankful for the two doors leading to my bedroom and the circular layout of the house, but only one of the two bedroom doors had a lock. What would I do? I heard Roy finally return to his bed fifteen minutes later and Clara asked, "What were you doing? Where were you?" Then, for the umpteenth time, she admonished, "You better behave yourself or the little girl is going to leave."

I quietly crept back to my bedroom. What could I do? I would definitely complain to Brenda first thing in the morning, but would he try sneaking in again that night? I could not even make myself get back into the bed after he had been in it, and I didn't fit under the bed, though I tried! My mother had worked to keep our home sheltered in many ways. Without television, movies, or any other previous exposure to inappropriate behavior of this sort, I reacted with a sort of shock. I spent the rest of the night sitting at the small table in my bedroom, too upset to sleep.

The next morning, Roy was unusually quiet, and after breakfast I slipped downstairs to call Brenda from the office before I left for church. I explained what happened and said, "I'm sorry, Brenda, but I really don't want to come back tonight unless there's a lock on that other door." She assured me they would install the lock on the door and would approach him if he tried any further mischief.

Two nights later, I woke up to hear him trying both doors. He fussed and spluttered when he found both doors locked, and when Clara asked him what was going on, she joined in the rumpus. The next day was Thanksgiving Day, but before I went home I called Brenda and told her I simply could not put up with this annoyance much longer. She once again assured me that they would approach Roy about his behavior, and I could only hope he would decide that bothering me was going to get him nowhere.

He was a quiet and sober man when I got back that evening, and he went to bed without saying a word. The next morning he brought some lame excuse, saying, "I only wanted to tell you how much I appreciate you coming to stay with us."

"Roy, I do not want to be told like that!"

"Arlene, I am an old man. I am not dangerous."

"That is beside the point! Behave or else!" I warned him again.

I felt I could not live with this constant tension, and I certainly was not happy working in this home. As I thought about how I felt and wondered what God expected me to do about it, I believe it was His Spirit who reminded me that although the situation was far from ideal, it was up to me to change my attitude. By always focusing on how I felt, I had allowed impatience and exasperation to take over. When I started thinking more about how I would want to be treated if I were in their shoes and looking for ways to bring joy to them, the unpleasantness did not go away, but God did give me a joy and sense of knowing I was at the right place at the right time. Still, I hoped that it would not be the right place for a long time!

Chapter 7

I shared my frustration with my friend Shirley, an aide at Goodwill Mennonite Nursing Home. When she told me about a job opening for a head cook at the home, I knew right away that I would love the work if my health allowed me to handle the stress of the job. On one hand, I truly believed that God could make it work if He wanted me to work there as I had given Him my life in every way I knew how. On the other hand, the odds looked like they were stacked pretty high against me. The nursing home was twenty miles from my home, and I had no vehicle, no driver's license, no place to live, and I still had undiagnosed health problems and some big questions about handling a full eight-hour shift.

God opened doors and windows that I had thought were sealed shut. Shirley offered me a home with her and her father, a widower. They then went the proverbial second mile, telling me not to worry about transportation. The nursing home was only two miles from their house, and Shirley's father volunteered as chauffeur until I was able to get my driver's license and a car.

I interviewed for the position and was hired on the spot. I would work only three days a week. Even that raised a question mark in my mind, but I was determined to give it a try.

My hunch proved true. I loved my work in the kitchen, but I was totally exhausted by the end of the shift. For extra income on my days off, I sat with an elderly couple who lived within walking distance. "No health, no wealth" I had always heard, and this certainly became true for me. In come cases, I lacked the money for my prescription drugs, and then the adage turned back on me to become "no wealth, no health." The doctor wanted to send me to have more tests done, but I could not see how my already strained budget would allow additional expenses.

My heart often echoed David's prayer to God: "O my God, . . . let not mine enemies triumph over me" (Psalm 25:2). I knew my old familiar enemies well, and they had envy-filled faces of self-pity and despair, wrinkled with worry lines. I longed to overcome these hateful enemies and stand solidly on the truth. My battle cry against my Goliath became, "I come against you in the name of the LORD Almighty, the God of the armies of Israel" (1 Samuel 17:45, NIV). Sometimes, however, I felt I could not even do battle but merely whispered the cry found in the Psalms: "Deliver me, O LORD, from mine enemies: I flee unto thee to hide me" (Psalm 143:9).

One morning when I went in to work, one of my co-workers asked if I was a relative of the Kauffman boy that drowned in Oakland the night before.

"What? From Oakland? No, I don't know anything about it."

Then another co-worker walked into the kitchen. "Hey, Arlene, did you hear about that fifteen-year-old boy that drowned in Oakland last night?"

Surely someone would have called us if he had been a relative of ours, but I could not shake the eerie feeling that hung over me as I dunked carrots into the water and scrubbed them absentmindedly. What if he was related to me? Who could it have been? Just to convince myself that all this worrying was nervous nonsense, I phoned home. They had not heard of the accident either. A few minutes later Mom called back.

"Arlene? For some reason, nobody got hold of us last night, but it was Galen."

Galen? My first cousin? Was it possible? I went through my shift in a haze. Somehow, through no special attention on my part, the food was distributed on the trays, separated into the gazillion specialized diets, and sent to the dining room. The eerie feeling stayed with me. Galen was one of my three cousins who passed away at the age of fifteen, and I had been extremely ill when I was fifteen. Jesse died after being infected with the AIDS virus from a blood transfusion. My cousin Sharon died with bone cancer at the knee after amputation and treatment failed. And now I received this terrible news about Galen.

I still remember laughing one day when Sharon came hobbling in the driveway sometime after the amputation and, impatient with her clunky wooden leg, unhooked it and came hopping toward the house on one leg. She had had such energy, such spirit. Now she was gone. And Galen was gone, too.

"This is a scary age," one of Sharon's sisters said, and I was beginning to agree.

The sun was lowering itself at the end of a long day when I came home from work and collapsed on my bed, bone tired and emotionally exhausted. Was it too much to ask God for strength for a normal eight-hour shift? I had not asked Him for a forty-hour week, and I did not even hope for lots of energy to spare, but why couldn't He give me enough for just three days a week? I buried my head in the soft pillow to stifle my sobs. *God, please, can't You do something? "Why, O Lord, do You hide Yourself in times of trouble?"*

As the first bursts of my sobbing subsided, I saw in my mind a picture of Jesus, His arms outstretched. Dressed in white light and coming through great clouds of white, He was welcoming me. I knew He was welcoming me, wanting me to come higher up and further in. The closer He came, the brighter and whiter the light. Suddenly, I saw only the nightstand and beyond that, the closet door. The fading light outside drifted dimly through the beige curtains. With the deep disappointment that I felt came a passionate longing for heaven. "Even so, come, Lord Jesus" (Revelation 22:20). I remembered some words from Isaiah: "In quietness and in confidence shall be your strength" (Isaiah 30:15).

These verses brought peace and rest as I felt my soul relaxing in the arms of God, and I fell asleep feeling that which could have come only from Him—warmth, security, and joy in knowing that my God had a purpose for my life.

The next morning, the nightstand and closet door were still there, but the vision was gone. Still, I held onto the memory of that gift from God, knowing that He is faithful and trustworthy and believing that someday things will be different. I still believe that, although it seems what James Conner writes is true: "Faith is a muscle, a diaphragm for breathing, and needs to be worked."[2]

Eventually, I was forced to quit my job at the nursing home due to my health. I felt I had walked on the road God had pointed toward only to find it a cul-de-sac. Following the Biblical admonition to "commit your way to the Lord; trust in him and he will do this" (Psalm 37:5, NIV) sounds like a good plan, but "committing" can be the hardest thing in the world.

Other people have made so many contributions to my life, and these months were no exception. Shirley and her father were wonderfully supportive, and I know he often worried about me when I was sick but thought I could not afford a visit to the doctor. Shirley had the intuition and sensitivity to pick up on my attitudes, particularly when my days looked like an unending string of blank spaces. More than once, she took me out for a day of writing fun memories on those blank spaces. These fun, relaxing times of sharing friendship helped me to get my mind off myself and my worries.

Marvette proved to be another true friend. One day she spoke up and said, "Arlene, I'll help you get your driver's license. How about it?"

"But, but, your new car?" I stuttered.

Marvette was a brave woman, and I got my driver's license after the second try.

On a stormy Sunday morning when church services were canceled for the day, my friend Kathy phoned, inviting me to their house for lunch and saying her dad had even offered to drive over the snowy roads to pick me up. We paged through some photo albums that afternoon, chatting and waiting out the storm. When I came to

2 Conner, James A., *Silent Fire*, Crown Publishers: New York, 2002, p. 26.

some photos of a bakery in Virginia where two of Kathy's sisters had worked, I exclaimed, "Oh, wouldn't I love to see a place like that!"

"Hey, you would really love to work there, wouldn't you?" one of them asked. "I'll call Sadie and talk to her. I don't know if she needs help or not."

"But could I?" I asked. "I mean, what if I can't work some days?"

"I don't know," she said. "I'll talk to Sadie and see what she says. It would be so perfect for you!"

Yes, I thought, *probably too perfect.* I had always wanted to work in a bakery, but it looked now like few of my wishes would ever come true. Still, what if this was God "directing my path"? The next weekend, Brenda and Orpha took me to Virginia to see the bakery and meet the owners.

As we neared our destination, I started feeling nervous. I am bashful and reserved around strangers and groups of people, although I sometimes wonder how introverted a woman can be after she has spent months in hospitals where strangers poke and pry and ask questions until there seem to be no secrets left.

Brenda and Orpha assured me I would love jolly, laughing Menno, his wife Sadie, and their family of seven lively girls. Their only son, a handicapped child, had passed away of leukemia when he was five years old, and four of the girls had moved out, leaving Brenda, Joann, and Barbara at home.

Stuarts Draft sits by the Blue Ridge Mountains in the lush, picturesque Shenandoah Valley. We stopped the car in front of a large house surrounded by a beautiful lawn with large maple trees and a white wooden fence. On the other side of the parking lot sat an empty trailer for the out-of-state bakery employees. At the front door, we were greeted with genuine southern hospitality.

"Come in! Come in!" Menno, I am sure, never met a stranger in his life, and I soon found he had a huge repertoire of jokes from which he could always pull one out to fit the occasion. His wife was more reserved, but I found she had a special gift of meeting others' practical needs, and that included serving up scrumptious, home-cooked meals.

After we enjoyed one of Sadie's feasts, she and I discussed the pros and cons of my coming to work in the bakery, and she told me she was willing to work with me and would adjust shifts as well as she could. She was so gentle, and her offer so generous, that I found myself wanting to do all I could to measure up to her expectations. I could hardly wait to see the bakery!

As we walked down the stairs into the ground level bakery, all was quiet, cool, and dark, closed up for the winter months. Sadie snapped on the lights, and I shivered with excitement as I walked through the bakery. Just seeing those huge 60-quart mixers, gigantic ovens, coolers, freezers and now-empty showcases convinced me that baking was in my blood.

While we traveled home, my mind went in circles. Could I do it? What if I couldn't?

"Arlene, you are quiet back there. What are you thinking?"

"What will I do if I get to Virginia and get sick again? The Kinsingers are busy in the bakery, and I don't want to get sick and dump myself into somebody's lap for care.

"Try it. I know they'll give you a fair trial," the girls assured me.

After thinking about it and asking God to continue leading my life, I decided to try taking the job. James offered to help me with moving, and I gladly accepted. Martha and I started comparing notes and, like sisters love to do, we put pieces together and decided that although James was a wonderful and caring brother, he might have had ulterior motives in wanting to make a trip to Virginia. Why else would he insist that Martha go along, that she bring her friend Joanna, and that we turn the trip into a weekend jaunt? We surely felt smart that we had seen through his plans and took lots of sisterly interest in the goings on between him and Joanna. Having pronounced Joanna a real sweetheart, we even cheerfully accepted the discomfort of traveling in crowded cars.

My cousin Saloma and her husband Junior, my only acquaintances in the community besides my new friends, the Kinsingers, showed much thoughtfulness and offered not only to have lunch ready when we arrived but to provide meals for the weekend. This would not be the only time Saloma appeared at my doorstep as an angel in disguise.

While I shopped for household items, the girls were looking at shoes. Joanna, a petite brunette who often needed to shop in the girls' section for shoes, was so excited when she found a ladies' shoe that fit her, but she didn't have enough cash with her to pay for them. James overheard and offered to pay for the shoes.

"I'll pay you back when I get home," Joanna assured him.

"Nah, that's okay. Just forget it."

Martha and I grinned at each other. James could not hide his secret from our sisterly intuition!

All too soon, however, they were pulling out of the driveway and heading back to Maryland. I was twenty-one years old with a job I knew I would love, but I still felt a twinge of loneliness as I watched them go.

Chapter 8

Kinsinger's Kountry Kitchen was open three days a week from March through December 24. When it first opened, the girls ranged in age from two to eighteen, and the whole family was involved. It was a bustling, jolly place where the whole family worked together, and their delicious baked goods made from scratch combined with the vibrant, cheerful atmosphere soon brought them quite a reputation in the community. We all soon came to recognize and love the regular customers. Some of the energetic girls found a way to combine fun with work and whizzed through the bakery on roller skates, making customers laugh while Sadie grinned and shook her head.

Tuesday was a day of preparation. Beginning at 8:00 a.m., we broke open 150 dozen eggs for cakes and cookies, cooked and peeled 50 to 70 pounds of potatoes for potato salad, cooked and peeled eggs for the salads, unwrapped 120 pounds of margarine, baked two turkeys and removed the meat for turkey salad, and measured ingredients for the next day. In the afternoon, two girls rolled out approximately 200 pie crusts for five different kinds of cream pie and egg custard pie. The crusts were put in the freezer and baked fresh daily as needed, and 110 fruit pies were frozen and taken out daily and baked as needed for the week.

On Wednesday mornings, Sadie was up and working by three o'clock, and when I arrived at five o'clock, there were already nine different kinds of cookies in the making and some were ready for me to package. That day, they also baked six kinds of cakes. German chocolate, carrot, and hummingbird cakes became my favorites.

Sadie asked me if I felt well enough to be at work again at five o'clock the next morning, and I was relieved that my body seemed to be taking the work all right. I always loved cooking and baking, so working here was like playing at my hobby on a large scale. I could only hope my strength and health would hold out.

Thursday was the opening day for the season, and I could hardly wait to see the business in full operation. I set the alarm clock for four o'clock a.m., but I was so excited I didn't even need it. The white and wheat breads were ready to put through the bread machine and out into pans, and the egg custard, shoo-fly, pecan, and fruit pies were already baked and ready to wrap.

I did most of the wrapping and bagging on the days we were open, and with a few brief rests throughout the day, I managed quite well. On Saturday evenings after the bakery closed, the employees were free to help themselves, although Sadie did sometimes take leftovers to the Salvation Army. I knew I needed to be careful with what I fed to my persnickety stomach, but I thought sometimes the delicious food was worth a little misery.

That weekend I called Mom, and when she informed me that James and Joanna were dating, I had to grin. This news was no surprise to me!

In June, I made a trip back home. Considering all the goodies Sadie loaded into my car, I was quite sure that especially Dad and my brothers, who all shared a notorious sweet tooth, would tell me to come home for visits often!

That summer, some friends from Maryland came to visit, and we had a jolly time chugging over the mountains in an old station wagon, visiting a pioneer farm where life in the 1800's was reenacted, chowing on watermelon, and eating up bakery leftovers. Another special memory-maker was the day my dear cousin Saloma and her husband took me and her sister Bertha to Natural Bridge for our birthdays. The wax museum was amazing, and the day was one I will always remember because of the love I felt from my friends.

Also in honor of my twenty-second birthday, a group of girls surprised me when they took me out for dinner. I made a foolish decision to treat myself and order what I most wanted to eat: a fried chicken sandwich with french fries. On top of my meal, the girls surprised me with a hot fudge cake with ice cream. It certainly was delicious, and I savored every bite, but I also paid for it that night. Saloma, concerned with how seriously upset my stomach became so quickly, recommended another visit to the doctor.

Dr. Riley ordered another batch of tests but still was unable to make a diagnosis concerning my abdominal pain. Although the story had been the same for nine years, my condition continued to worsen. Dr. Riley, like others before him, prescribed different medications to relieve my pain, but I experienced no improvement. Still, I was able to work fairly consistently in the bakery, and I still enjoyed my work. The other employees often talked about the exploding business the holidays brought in November and December, and in October the bakery ordered 10,000 pounds of flour to last through the next two months.

The Kinsingers had an annual tradition for the first week in November, when they kicked off the holiday season for their customers with a grand chicken barbecue in the parking lot. Menno cooked old-fashioned apple butter in a large open kettle on an open fire, and, of course, the entire shindig was a big hit.

After this weekend, the bakery featured the seasonal specialties. During the week of Thanksgiving, we baked between 800 and 900 pumpkin pies for the three days when the bakery was open. For Christmas, fresh coconut cakes were best sellers, and on December 23 of the year I was working there, 150 were sold, followed with fruitcakes, cranberry salad and mincemeat pies.

Going to bed late and rising at one or two o'clock in the morning was beginning to wear on "Mama Sadie." One day her daughters attacked her and declared, "You are going for a nap!" One of the girls took her by her legs and another took her by her upper body, and they carried her off up the stairs, with Sadie fighting the whole way. After tucking her in bed nice and snug, the girls closed the door and piled furniture in front of the door. They descended the stairs, chuckling to themselves and feeling self-satisfied, certain there was no way of escape. Turning around, who should they see but their mother. Exasperated, they asked, "Mom, it is impossible to get you down for a nap. How did you get out?"

It was Sadie's turn to feel smug. "I looked up and down the road to make sure nobody was looking, then I quickly crawled out the window and went around the house, in through the bakery, and back upstairs in time to watch you block off the door. What a waste of time." Sadie chuckled and shook her head at them.

While we were busy with holiday orders, my bouts of pain and nausea were growing more frequent, even without chicken and fries! After a particularly rough night, I called Dr. Riley for another appointment. He was out of town, but his replacement, Dr. Neal, almost immediately declared that when people complain of stomach problems, the stomach is not usually the source of their pain. "I'm 99% positive you're having gallbladder trouble. It won't always show up on tests if there aren't any stones. Where do you want to go for a surgeon?"

"Let me think about it," I told him. My strength and energy were dwindling, but I badly wanted to stick it out until Christmas Eve. After ten years of undiagnosed problems, could the answer be as easy as removing a gallbladder? "Doctor, I also still have chest pains and palpitations that started when I was in elementary school, and they seem to be getting worse. And I'm constantly tired."

"I would suggest you see a cardiologist sometime before you go in for surgery," he said. He still seemed convinced he had discovered my real problem and insisted on setting up the appointment for me.

Oh, but I hoped and prayed he was right in his diagnosis. After more than ten years of intermittent pain and constant exhaustion, it stretched my imagination to think what a normal life would be like. What all had I missed in those years just by being so tired? I go to bed tired and wake up tired. It is a form of fatigue unknown to healthy, busy people who know only the exhaustion that comes after a day of energetic work.

I went for more tests, by now convinced that they soon would have catalogued and graphed every inch of my body and its processes. After the results came back to the cardiologist, he called me with the report that I did have a mitral valve prolapse and an irregular heartbeat. He prescribed medication to help with my chest pains and irregular heartbeat, warning me that many medical procedures, including dental work, would require that I take antibiotics beforehand.

Two days later I was experiencing extreme exhaustion and felt I could not possibly work. The bakery was busy, and I felt so helpless, knowing that healthy people see the work that needs to be done and often do not understand limitations like mine. During their busiest times, vehicles filled the parking lot and extended down the road in both directions. Two hours before opening time, anxious customers had formed a line, and the bakery could scarcely afford to be short staffed. Sometimes I wondered how far and how long I could actually push myself. I called the doctor, and he told me to discontinue one of the medications I was taking. After the Inderal had cleared out of my system, he prescribed a new medication with better success.

The week of Christmas, the Kinsinger family lived in the bakery. They rounded up all the help they could find, and the entire extended family was involved. By Christmas Eve, everybody was dragging. On Christmas morning Sadie called and invited me over for Christmas dinner. The children were live wires filled with Christmas excitement, but the adults were slumped over, sleeping on the floor, on easy chairs, or wherever they had chanced to drop. I have no idea where dear Sadie got all her energy, but she prepared a genuine Christmas dinner with all the fixings.

As I anticipated surgery, I wondered if I had set my hopes too high. Was it realistic to think that perhaps my physical problems would be solved with my gallbladder removal? In January, 1988, I went to see Dr. Ringer, a highly recommended Maryland doctor majoring in gallbladder surgeries. I was almost shocked when, without a second thought, he agreed that my gallbladder was the problem. "Unless there are stones, it often doesn't show up on X-rays. We take out the gallbladder and the patients feel great!" he said with confidence.

Chapter 9

Two weeks later, he removed my gallbladder through a five-inch incision. Recovery went well until twenty-four hours after surgery, when an unexplainable, severe abdominal pain attacked me mercilessly.

"Here is a rocking chair, Arlene. If this is trapped gas, maybe rocking will shift those air pockets and relieve the pain," the nurse suggested.

I rocked and writhed but found no relief. The movement only made me hurt worse.

Three days after surgery, the doctor came in, sat down on the wide window sill, and looked at me without saying a word.

"Tell me what's happening," I pleaded. Tears ran down my cheeks from the terrible, unrelenting pain pinching and knifing my stomach.

"Arlene, I don't know what to do," he said helplessly. "We'll try to keep your pain tolerable, but pain is a danger signal. If we completely suppress the pain, we might miss something we need to know about. Obviously, something's going on, but I don't know what."

"Lord? Lord? I need You . . . I need You." The groans and prayers went together. The knowledge that He knew what was happening to me and that someday it would be all right somehow got me through those long days. Six long days later, the pain was no longer constant but had reduced itself to coming in attacks.

Rather than spending three days in the hospital, I was there for ten days. This was not a promising start; I had hoped to have my surgery done and be recuperated in March when the bakery opened. As time went on, the pain lessened. The attacks became less frequent until I came to expect them four or fives times daily, and they often lasted fifteen to thirty minutes. The attacks brought severe pain, but between the attacks, I felt better than I had for years. I was amazed that a person could feel so good! I also found that I did not need to be as cautious with my diet, although in retrospect, I wonder if staying with a strict diet would have helped me in the long run. Six weeks after surgery, I felt I was doing well enough that I headed back to my home in Virginia, where I found I was still weaker than I thought.

Before I had gone to Maryland for surgery, Mary Jane Miller, a cousin to Dad, had called and offered me work in their suspender shop while I was still recuperating. They were looking for more help but did not need me to stay on a strict schedule.

Eli and Mary Jane had worked at a children's home in Germany for some years. After they had adopted Dorothea from Germany, Rosie from Turkey, and Nathaniel from El Salvador, Eli became ill with crippling arthritis. Needing to provide for his family in spite of his disability, they opened Shenandoah Valley Sales, a suspender-making business. It was a project Eli was able to do until his hands became too crippled, and the business grew until it provided adequate income to support the family. After battling with arthritis for more than twelve years, Eli suddenly passed away as a result of a heart attack, leaving Mary Jane with a business to run and three teenage children to care for.

I quickly fell in love with Mary Jane, a strong, compassionate woman. I decided to work in the suspender shop until the bakery opened or until I had the strength to work in the bakery. The suspender shop was perfectly suited to my needs. I could work as much as I wanted to work and as long as I wanted to work. The tasks were easy, and Mary Jane's experience with her husband's illness gave her a compassion and understanding few people acquire in spite of their good hearts.

"Don't push yourself, dear. Just work at your own pace; the suspenders won't burn like those cakes at the bakery," she would say.

Not everybody knows what real pain is, so to avoid emotional pain, I sometimes hide in my shell, trying hard to appear normal to prevent others from knowing about my pain. Sometimes people assumed I was not as bad off as I "pretended" to be. On the other hand, I sometimes found people who appeared overly protective and stifling. "Now, now, let me do that for you," or "Now, now, you should go rest." Tsk, tsk, tsk!

My cousin Saloma continued to be an angel with a very thin disguise. Although she was busy with work on the farm and caring for her young family, she always surprised me with her sensitivity to my needs and with all the ways she cared for me while helping me do all I was reasonably able to do. Many summer evenings when the Virginia heat turned my trailer into an oven, Saloma and her husband welcomed me to join them where they often ate outside under their gazebo.

In May 1988, I had the chance to travel to Delaware with my cousin Bertha and her family to visit my grandparents, whom I had not seen for three years. The heat presented a concern for me, for they were Amish and did not have electricity. Consequently, there was no air conditioning or fans. Any traveling at all raised questions about my low store of energy, unpredictable medical problems, and intermittent abdominal pain. I thought I could not pen myself up forever out of fear of what might happen, so I chose to make the trip, deciding that if worse came to worst, Delaware had hospitals too.

The thermometer read 100° F in the shade when we arrived in Delaware. Aunt Laura stoked the fire in the old fashioned cookstove in the kitchen and asked me and Bertha to prepare lunch while the others held a family meeting concerning care for Grandpa's. Neither one of us had any experience with cookstoves, but that stove radiated more heat than the hot sand in the Sahara! Bertha put some potatoes on the stove to cook, then helped me shell some freshly picked peas from the garden.

Suddenly, Bertha squealed and her brown eyes opened wide. "The potatoes are boiling over! What do I do? I can't turn the burner down!

Do I have to put out the fire in the stove?" My cousins and I doubled over laughing at our predicament.

"It's not funny! What am I supposed to do?" she asked, perturbed at our lack of helpfulness. Eventually, we had the food prepared and the table set.

The heat and the mosquitoes made the night miserable, but I never regretted visiting my grandparents. It was the last time I saw them, and I was unable to attend either of their funerals two years later because both times I was recuperating from pancreatitis.

That September I traveled to Maryland for James and Joanna's wedding. The drive over the mountains turned out to be a special time alone, and the splendor of the autumn foliage turned my mind and heart toward God. I think sometimes He brings these moments of clarity, joy, and beauty so that I have something to hold onto when life looks like a continuous mess.

Joanna had stowed away the pair of shoes James had bought for her in Virginia and wore them on her wedding day. Dad did attend the wedding, though he tried to remain unnoticed on the balcony. He and James had often worked together, and a special bond had developed between them. James and Joanna had a lovely autumn wedding, and it brought me happiness to see my brother so delighted, even while I wondered if marriage would ever be something I could enjoy. I knew already that God's plan for my life did not look like His plan for many of my friends, but the last chapter was not yet written.

Menno walked into the bakery one day to talk to me. "Arlene, every two years we take a trip to Florida during winter break. This year only Joann and Barbara will be coming along, but you've been with us for two years, and we'd like to take you along as a daughter. It'll be a free trip for you."

I was shocked speechless for a moment. "Menno! I can hardly believe what I'm hearing! I'd love to go, of course, but I'll have to think about it for a little." This was a once-in-a-lifetime opportunity for me, but I needed to be realistic. I was a poor traveler, I tired easily, I was still prone to getting attacks of abdominal pain, and I did not like the idea of being an inconvenience to Menno's family. Still, if all went well. . . .

My family and friends encouraged me to go, and I decided to go for it. So in January of 1989, I was on my way to Florida. We loaded up and pulled out onto the highway, driving through dense fog and darkness. We had been on the road for only an hour when Menno, who had put in a long day of work, started fighting sleep. I was relieved when he pulled off to the side of the road and almost immediately fell asleep, so I watched the traffic and felt more bored and restless by the minute. I was already tired of traveling, and here we sat, only one hour's drive from home! A nap helped Menno, and we were on the way again, but sleep would not come even though my eyes felt thick and heavy. Eventually, the long night ended and the sun appeared. After a long fourteen hours, we arrived in Tennessee where we met Sadie, who had been visiting some of her family.

After a good weekend in Tennessee, we headed for Florida. I now had quite a lively bunch of traveling companions. Menno teased and cracked jokes as usual while Joann and Barbara, restless and full of pent up energy, tussled. Sadie, always the mother, kept watch over them all. And I sat watching them with a grin on my face.

Driving through Florida, we began seeing acres upon acres of sugar cane and large orchards full of citrus fruit. And that was the beginning of a week of new sights for me. We took a wooden boat through the jungle and got to watch zebras, water buffalo, monkeys, and other jungle creatures along the river.

"What is the difference between a male and a female zebra?" Menno asked, then answered himself with a chuckle: "The male is black and white and female is white and black."

Going out on a glass bottom boat showed me a whole new world of beauty as I saw yet another dimension of the world God created. It convinced me that God loves beauty, and I felt surrounded by gifts of beauty from Him. Already, I was so glad I had come along to Florida, for I knew it was not likely I would be able to make a trip like this again. I hoped the pain I had would stay under control until we got back, and I was sure Mom and my friends were praying that I could enjoy this trip.

Joann and Barbara rented three-wheeled bikes and soon persuaded me to join them, though I had little faith in my biking skills. Soon they even had a slightly worried Menno riding around and admitting it was "a little" fun. Only Sadie could not be budged, sticking to her determined refusal. She would not get on one of those things.

My pain continued to worsen throughout that week although it had not yet become unbearable. My worry, however, threatened to turn the trip rotten. What would I do if I needed medical help? Over and over I reminded myself that I had done all I could; if I got sick, I knew my Father in heaven knew what was going on and had allowed it.

Florida is full of attractions for tourists like me, and I loved exploring Jungle Larry's African Safari with its lively animal shows and exhibits, the Everglades, Key West, the Cypress Gardens, and Sea World. We took an airboat over Safari Park to see more wildlife, and while flying through the air, Menno was in his glory! I decided he could have all the alligators he wanted; I hardly even liked looking at their dreadful mouths.

I even survived the drive home, almost to my surprise! Truly, though, this wonderful vacation was a beautiful gift both from God and from Menno and Sadie, and it is one I will always remember with thankfulness. I could not have known then what a bright spot these memories would be in the darkness of the following months.

Chapter 10

In March, the pain that had been threatening for months finally broke through the surface. This time the agonizing pain did not let up. I paced the floor that night, rocked back and forth, and curled into a tight ball. Nothing brought relief. At 3:30 a.m. I finally called Sadie, who was already in the bakery. The pain gripped my insides, arresting my breath and making it hard even to speak, although I tried to sound normal. "Sadie, I'm hurting, and I need someone to take me to Little Rock."

"I'm not sure what's causing your pain," the doctor admitted. "All the tests taken came back normal. Who is your family doctor?"

"Dr. Riley," I answered.

"As soon as his office opens in the morning, call him. We need to become more aggressive to find out what's going on."

Does Jesus care? The rocky path of illness I was stuck on looked hopeless. Sometimes God's greatest mercies are His refusals, I've heard. But I longed for an explanation, a few sentences written on the wall, perhaps, declaring the perfect will of God. Perhaps God knows that if He would provide an explanation, I still would not understand. Yet He asks me to trust.

When Dr. Riley came in, he seemed alarmed. "I'm going to make arrangements to have an EGD done. You had one of these done a number of years ago. It's when we put a small tube down your throat and into the stomach to check for ulcers or any other possible source of irritation." I am sure I did not look impressed. "We'll sedate you, so it shouldn't be too bad," he said.

Saloma once again showed what could only have been a piece of divine love. "Arlene, I'll get a babysitter, then I can take you for your

EGD in the morning."

I protested, knowing she was a busy mother and farm wife. But she was right; I didn't have family close by. "Arlene, I want to support you in the best way I know," she said. I still thank God for giving me someone like Saloma.

After the EGD, the doctor reported that he found inflammation in the stomach lining but believed the problem lay farther down than he could see with the short scope. "I'd like to refer you to Dr. Allen, a gastrointestinal doctor at the university hospital in Charles Town.

Dear Saloma took me to Charles Town for my appointment with Dr. Allen. I was checked in at the front desk, and then we waited, not one or two hours, but three hours, until I was finally called in only to have a student doctor ask many of the same questions over again. Again we waited. I was ready for a rest, and I am sure Saloma was ready to get home to take care of her children.

When Dr. Allen finally came in, he did not beat around the bush. "If this is the peculiar problem we think it is, we know little about it. We appreciate people like you who allow us to learn more about this illness—although I am certain you didn't choose this problem," he added with a small grin. "Fortunately, Dr. Ohler here in Charles Town is one of the three top experts in the nation who are researching this field. We'd like to schedule you for an ERCP. Hopefully, that will give us some answers. ERCP stands for 'endoscopic retrograde choledochopancreatography,' but in short and blunt terms, it is 'the long scope.'" I decided that did not sound promising at all.

On the way home I told Saloma, "I declare, I feel like a genuine guinea pig in a research lab! If it's going to be profitable to me or to others, I can consent, but you never know." It was a mercy I had no idea of what would come in the years still ahead of me.

My alarm clock rang early on the morning of my meeting with that ominous-sounding "long scope." I looked across the parking lot toward the bakery, and I felt troubled as I thought of how much I would have enjoyed being in the bakery. I had not been able to work regularly, and I was sensing that some misunderstandings had arisen. I knew I tried hard to appear normal and, to avoid emotional pain, I chose not to open up unless I knew someone was genuinely concerned. Even then, I hated the thought of being a whining, sickly person with many troubles and ailments.

It was springtime, and the drive to Charles Town was beautiful and brought peace as I tried not to think about where I was going and why. After arriving at the hospital, I was amazed at how relaxed I felt and knew it could only be because of God's love.

They needed to do the ERCP close to an X-ray room so they could snap pictures as they performed the procedure. I wondered how many students would pore over photos of my digestive tract. It appeared I was going to be the center of attraction and education as one person after the other came into the room.

A middle-aged man with thinning black hair walked toward me. "Arlene?" he asked, shaking my hand.

"Yes," I answered. I liked Dr. Ohler right away. His blue eyes twinkled, and his smile was genuine and kind. He explained to me what he expected to find and, following medical protocol, warned me of the possible risks, including pancreatitis, irritation, and bleeding. He believed there was a restriction in the area where the liver, gallbladder, and pancreas join, called the common bile duct. They had only a few cases on record of high pressures in this duct, but I thought that made sense; I always seemed to be one of the "few cases," my problems written in the small print of what might happen but probably wouldn't.

"The scope is passed down through the esophagus, stomach, small intestines and on through until we finally come to the common bile duct for a study. Then we pass a fine flexible tube through the scope, injecting dye through the biliary system, which shows any abnormalities in the ducts on the X-ray films. Depending on what we find, we can take care of it while we are in there. If there are stones causing an obstruction, they can be removed by attaching a device on the scope to widen the duct. If there is a tumor, we can perform a biopsy at the same time."

After all the preparations were made, I was wheeled into the room. The medical staff was obviously much more excited than I was. Again I dared to hope and pray this would give us the answers we needed to fix my troublesome body.

Karen, my nurse, assured me that the sedative they gave through my IV would relax me, and I would remember nothing of the procedure. I certainly hoped she was right.

"Okay, we're going to spray some anesthetic into your throat to numb the throat and esophagus. I warn you, it's not very tasty stuff. Open wide." I started wretching, and I was sure I was going to suffocate. They sprayed the dreadful stuff into my throat three times, and it was one of the most horrid experiences I've had.

"Did you ever taste this stuff?" I asked Karen.

"No, and I hope I never need to."

I thought any nurse who endured some of these things before graduation would be more considerate and understanding. When I saw that stiff black tube, as thick as my thumb and called a "scope," I almost croaked. "Wait! I am still awake and I have to swallow that thing?"

"We can't sedate you too heavily until you swallow it, but we'll give you some more medication. You don't go down easily!" Dr. Ohler said, "Give her two more."

Forty-five minutes later they pulled out the scope, and I fell into a deep sleep, forty-five minutes too late. They had given me eight doses of the anesthesia instead of the normal two, but it had taken too long for it to take hold. I had been awake for the whole procedure and could feel that awful tube moving in my stomach. Never again did I want to go through that experience.

On the way home, Saloma handed me some bad news. They had been unable to complete the study due to complications with my heart and my dangerously low blood pressure. "As far as they could see," she said, "everything looked normal, so they have even more reasons to believe it is pressure in the bile ducts further down."

My heart sank, and I closed my eyes against the tears. All that mis-

ery and still no answers. "Now what?" I asked her.

"He wants to see you in the office in two weeks," Saloma answered. She did not mention another ERCP, but deep inside I suspected that was what she meant. I tried as hard as I could to convince myself I was wrong. I could not face that type of misery again.

Chapter 11

The medical staff had told me that if I was going to get pancreatitis from the procedure, I would have had it before I left the hospital, but at nine o'clock that night I started to hurt like I had never hurt before. I had thought my earlier abdominal pain was nearly unbearable, but this torment was beyond that. My whole body tingled and my vision blurred. I have heard that chronic pancreatitis is one of the most painful illnesses known, an assertion I do not doubt for one minute.

Menno and Sadie took me to Charles Town, where they were expecting my arrival. I moaned and groaned and this time did not even care if the world thought I was wimpy. Every bump in the road brought new torture, and I could see my belly was actually expanding.

"Arlene, are you doing okay back there?" Menno asked.

"Can't you go a little faster?"

"I'm already going over the speed limit, but I'll push it a little more."

Immediately after I arrived at the emergency room, they drew blood and took me for X-rays. "Where is the pain?" the doctor asked as he laid his cold hands on my stomach and pressed gently. My reflexes reacted, and I grabbed his hands, involuntarily pulling up my legs.

"That hurts so much," I gasped.

"I'm sorry," he apologized.

I answered questions very briefly, for even the effort of speaking increased my discomfort. Eventually the tests were returned, verifying I had pancreatitis resulting from the ERCP procedure done early that afternoon. Pancreatitis is essentially inflammation of the pancreas as pancreatic tissue is eaten up by the pancreas's own enzymes. Often caused by alcoholism or biliary tract disease, pancreatitis can also be set off by abdominal trauma, and obviously the ERCP could be categorized as "abdominal trauma."

After they finally got their ducks in a row and their charts filled out, I was admitted to the hospital and given morphine for better pain control. Since this was the first time I had pancreatitis, they limited the pain medication until they knew for certain what caused it. I felt terrible frustration. They could have by-passed this if they had only talked to Dr. Ohler. Never again would this happen; I would rather die than go through another ERCP experience and the agony of pancreatitis.

I knew God would not give me any more than I could bear with His mercy, but in my low times the enemy and destroyer of souls did his best to make me believe God was taking it a bit too far. I am convinced that the people who prayed for me in those times when I could no longer pray for myself served as God's protection from the enemy, who always lurked nearby with his lies and despair.

The night held even more difficulties. My bladder was full, and I couldn't void. I explained my problem to the nurse, who shortly said that they needed a doctor's orders to catheterize me and that he was seeing patients in the office. "There's no reason you shouldn't be able to do it on your own," she added.

"But I tried. . . ." They still paid no attention. Why, why, why did I need to suffer so unnecessarily? When Saloma walked in the door, I thought for the hundredth time I was seeing an angel. When I told her my bladder was about to burst and they were doing nothing about it, she marched down to Dr. Ohler's office and told him what was going on.

"What's he doing about it?" I asked Saloma when she came back.

"He was pretty upset, and he's putting in an order now."

After Dr. Ohler gave the orders, the nurse drained more than a liter from my bladder. The first three days, I had nothing to eat or drink.

Then I started on ice chips and moved to liquids like Jell-O, broth, and juice. Meal after meal was the same: Jell-O, broth, and juice until I thought that alone was enough to make me sick.

"No appetite?" the doctor asked, punching his finger into the Jell-O sitting by my bed.

"No." Hospital food left much to be desired without doctors poking their fingers into it. This reminded me of the time when I was eleven years old and Mom had taken James for treatment. Alton and I did the cooking if Dad was not around, and we both had our regular choices of food. Alton often made rice, his personal favorite. My favorite was graham cracker fluff.

"Alton, not rice again," whined David. "We never have anything else when Mom isn't at home. Always rice and graham cracker fluff. I can't wait till Mom comes home again!"

"Me too, me too." Apparently the rest of them agreed.

Each nurse, each floor, and each hospital seems to have its own reputation. Some nurses are prompt while others cause needless suffering. "Oh, I forgot," or "sorry, I was on break," or "I was busy" are often careless excuses. One of my favorite nurses told me once that I'm not demanding enough to get the care I really need, but I knew patients quickly develop reputations for themselves, too. I really want people who see me to recognize that I am different because I am a servant of Jesus, and I still hate the idea of being a complainer.

I had both kind, thoughtful nurses and some who were there for the money. One nurse was particularly bad. Clara informed me regularly that she saw no reason why I should have been admitted to the hospital after an ERCP. "It's been ten days and you still say you aren't ready to go home?" she asked. It was the doctor who ultimately made those decisions; it was not me and it certainly was not the nurse.

After two weeks, I was sent home on "liquids as tolerated." Before I went home, the doctor informed me that X-rays had shown an ovarian cyst and fibroid tumors in the uterus, so I knew that I needed to get well enough to come back to the hospital. I could not help being glad I could not see very far down the road of my future. But I was equally glad that I knew Someone who did see it and who would be there.

The day I was discharged, Saloma came to pick me up. Clara was on duty again, and the discharge papers were completed. I was dressed and, knowing that hospital rules require staff to take discharged patients out on wheelchairs, I sat and waited for Clara to bring me a wheelchair. She passed outside the door, caught a glimpse of me, then came back and asked what I was waiting for.

"We are waiting for a wheelchair," Saloma answered.

"There is no reason she can't walk out of this hospital. She could if she'd only make up her mind." Clara did finally bring us a wheelchair, but Saloma had to wheel me out. On the way out, we stopped and talked to the receptionist, who took my name, room number, and the name of the nurse. I hate to get others into trouble, but I wondered how many patients she was treating the way she had treated me. Nobody, healthy or ill, should need to deal with nurses like that.

Sometimes I think of how I would love being a nurse. Having lived the hospital life for so long, I would delight in the challenge of doing all the little things that only a patient would notice to make people more comfortable. One of my nurses complained that because of the hospital being understaffed she could never spend quality time with her patients, and this kept her from feeling fulfilled and successful at her job. I am convinced she was right that a friendly smile, a caring touch, and a kind word hold extraordinary healing power. Negative nurses likewise hold power to impact their patients.

About two months later, I again went in to see Dr. Ohler. On the way over, I told Saloma not to let them persuade me to do another ERCP unless they promised to fully sedate me. And if I got pancreatitis the second time, I did not know if I could take it.

After explaining what he understood about my situation, Dr. Ohler finally admitted that he could see no way to get around doing another ERCP. He promised to try another drug combination to guarantee better results with the anesthesia and to do all he could to prevent pancreatitis. Whether it was out of stupidity, stubbornness, or desperation, I don't know, but I signed the consent form. I knew I was holding onto the promise that my God would be with me. And, yes, I still hoped for a miracle.

> Even though I walk
> through the valley of the shadow of death,
> I will fear no evil,
> for you are with me;
> your rod and your staff,
> they comfort me (Psalm 23:4, NIV).

Saloma became a safe person for me to confide in about those things that were bothering me, and her presence brought added security in a way that made me feel she truly was Jesus' hands and feet. With all my health problems and physical discomfort, it was important for me to have a friend who cared. I also knew I would soon need to give up the job I enjoyed so much, and I knew relationships back home were strained. They reported that Dad, a quiet and closed man, seemed to have something on his mind that he refused to talk about. Saloma listened and cared about my heart, and we talked as we drove to Charles Town for ERCP #2.

The horrible procedure was completed, and once again they had been unable to put me to sleep completely. Unfortunately, it was as bad as I had remembered, but this time I hoped it was not totally futile. Dr. Ohler almost bounded into my room, obviously excited about something. "Arlene, we found the problem! I have never heard of pressures measuring that high in the common bile duct anywhere in the Nation." I hoped that also meant he had answers. I did not think topping the charts was an accomplishment!

The Short Stay Unit at the hospital was closing up for the day, and Dr. Ohler once again declared I would not get pancreatitis if I was not already showing any signs of it. After a long day, we headed home. I was aware of the sacrifices that Saloma's family made in her absence.

At ten o'clock, I saw I was not going to escape pancreatitis this

time, either. "Oh no, not you!" the dismayed nurse exclaimed after she saw who I was. Oh, honey, I am so sorry." Of course, she needed to draw blood and get an IV started for the first thing. I was notorious for my bad veins, and they often worked and worked, pricking over and over again, before they got into the vein. As she worked, she said, "You're a bit dehydrated, and that's not helping any."

"Why shouldn't I be dehydrated? I didn't have anything by mouth for nearly twenty-six hours."

When the blood work results came back, I was admitted to the hospital with pancreatitis. I wished they could just take my word for it and put me on morphine before their tests told them what I knew. The agony of pancreatitis is hard to describe because when the worst pain one knows gets worse, words no longer work.

Chapter 12

As I was recuperating between the episodes of pancreatitis, I tried to help in the bakery the best I could, but I came home bone tired and stressed out. In spite of my efforts to keep up with the bakery work and hide how poorly I felt, I knew some people were wondering if I really was as sick as I thought I was. It seemed that whether I minimized my pain or was truthful about it, I could not escape having some people see me as complaining and lazy. Often, the problem is just that healthy people cannot really understand what life is like for those of us who have not been given the gift of health.

I had grown up learning to work. Picking up toys, setting the table, washing dishes, sweeping floors, gathering diapers from the wash line—the list of things we children could do grew as we grew. Mom made a chart and assigned daily chores to each of us. We got a star for doing a job well, two stars for seeing and doing a job without being told. Even on mornings before I left for school, I helped with laundry and punched down Mom's bread dough. Every two days I had sixty or more diapers to hang out on the wash line. Certainly, I sometimes complained, but this was no child labor boot camp. We had learned to appreciate the satisfying feeling of a job well done, and I liked to see Mom's laundry flapping on the wash line when I went to school. Hard work brought me a sense of fulfillment, and I enjoyed learning to do new things. Now I could not work, and my illness meant I needed to deal with unspoken questions from people who often did not know me well.

I had been having problems with low blood pressure caused by the medication they used to mitigate the pressure in my common bile duct. At my next appointment with Dr. Ohler, he verified my worst fears. I was facing another ERCP. Since my blood pressure problems would not allow them to give me enough medication to relieve the pressure, they wanted to go in and snip the sphincter to relieve the pressure.

The heat in the bakery and in the trailer were oppressive, and even though kindhearted Menno surprised me by installing an air conditioner in the trailer, I knew if this sphincterotomy did not take care of the problem, I would need to leave the bakery. Hope is sometimes irrational, and I was still crazy enough to hope that this time my problem would be fixed.

Oh, Lord, I am Yours. Give me not what seems best but what is best. I am Your creation and Your daughter. I can't just walk away from my problems, so make them something beautiful for Your honor. I desperately need You, and I just can't do it alone.

On June 21, 1989, I went in for my third ERCP in four weeks. The day before the ERCP, Saloma and I had a big baking day to stock her freezer with cookies. We also took the nurses at the Short Stay Unit some pumpkin whoopie pies, and it was great fun to see their delight. We were learning to know them on a more personal level, and I had found that the more personal I as a patient seemed, the better treatment I received.

It was difficult to submit to another ERCP, but Dr. Ohler declared it absolutely necessary, and I did not know where I could go if I chose not to follow his advice. "There will be no dye involved and no manipulation, so I see no reason at all why you should get pancreatitis. I know I told you all that before, but I'll do my best."

I guess I don't learn from unrealistic positive thinking. I again hoped.

This time, they kept me in the hospital overnight for observation and to make sure there was no internal bleeding from the cut they made. Poor Dr. Ohler was totally frustrated, but I had been awake again to feel that hard tube with its scope searching through my stomach. Soon I began vomiting and suffering severe pain. I knew all too well what was happening. I called the nurse and explained I was getting pancreatitis and was in terrible pain.

"It isn't pancreatitis—you don't even have a fever," the nurse said, making no effort to get me something for pain control. All night, I tried to convince them differently. After two major episodes, I should know! Nothing else hurt like this. Writhing all night and feeling helpless frustration with the nursing staff totally drained me emotionally. In the morning, after the doctor was in, they got blood work done and proved me right. It was a pretty hard pill for the nurse to swallow.

After they got the morphine going, I finally had some relief. Then my roommate turned up her television, and every thumping beat of the music she was listening to sent darts of pain through my abdomen. What sort of horrid person was she?

"Ma'am, your roommate is very sick! You need to turn down your TV!" my nurse told her. The roommate turned out not to be the ogre she first seemed to be, and she actually had a caring heart. A few times, she called out to the nurses' desk and complained that they weren't bringing me morphine when I needed it.

Dr. Ohler's colleague, who was covering for him in the hospital, sat down beside me on the bed. "You seem to be coping well. You've obviously got Someone on your side looking after you, and it sure makes our job a pleasure. You can't imagine what we see in some patients. They get demanding and expect us to make their lives perfect. Your patience and happiness is totally amazing." His words were music to my ears. I longed for people to see the difference Jesus made in my life. "Not that we are sufficient of ourselves to think any thing as of ourselves; but our sufficiency is of God" (2 Corinthians 3:5). Sometimes I thought showing other people Jesus in suffering was my only purpose in life.

Two weeks later, I was discharged to continue recuperating. Since they had cut the sphincter, the pressure seemed to lessen and the pain with it. Oh, but I hoped it was the final solution! During this time of recovery, it became clear that the bakery was not keeping up with its work. The holiday season was approaching, and Sadie felt that if they could not find more help, they would need to close the business. I had sensed it coming to this, and it made me feel awful. I had so badly wanted to be a dependable worker, but I also realized I had done what I could and needed to give Sadie the freedom to find other employees.

This meant I needed to find another place to live. I could not just move back to Maryland because I didn't want to drive five hours for every visit with Dr. Ohler, and I knew of no other doctors close to Maryland with his expertise. I drove over to talk to my dear friend Saloma.

"Maybe if you go to Maryland this weekend, something else will turn up," she said.

"But what?" I asked. The sphincterotomy seemed to have helped, and I was definitely feeling better again, but I probably couldn't even flip burgers if I wanted to. The doctor had warned me that all the work they had done left me with scar tissue that could cause new complications with little warning. I needed to face the facts: my illness was chronic. No flip of a wand or scalpel would fix my problems now.

Chapter 13

Driving over the mountains to Maryland that weekend provided good "alone time" for thinking, but my mind just threw out questions and doubts. Even if Dr. Howard in Maryland agreed to take on my case, which up to this point he had avoided, could I trust him the way I did Dr. Ohler? Where would I work? Where would I live? When would I ever find a job that could flex with my unpredictable body? Why was this necessary? I knew the "right" answers: God uses the school of life and suffering to teach and train me. Teaching and training me for what? I sometimes asked with the other side of my mind.

"Consider it pure joy, my brothers, whenever you face trials of many kinds, because you know that the testing of your faith develops perseverance" (James 1:2, 3, NIV). It all sounded like some insane joke, as though I was a guinea pig in God's hospital, too. God's ways were beyond me, but still I wanted to know Him, wanted to love Him, wanted to trust Him. He had, after all, given me a promise: "If any of you lacks wisdom, he should ask God, who gives generously to all without finding fault, and it will be given to him" (James 1:5, NIV).

Sunday morning in my home church, my eyes widened and my mind started spinning when they announced that the family of Barbara Yoder was looking for someone to move in with her as soon as possible. Barbara was a stroke victim and had lost her speech. *I'm not ready for that, Lord!* Conflicting voices clamored in my head all through the service. Finally, I told God I would at least inquire about the work. I did not get to speak to any of the family that morning, but at the second service, the usher led me to the pew in front of Chad and Pauline. Chad was Barbara's son, and I thought that apparent coincidence must have actually been planned by God.

After the last amen, I turned around to talk to them. I asked more about the job and told them I was looking for something. They knew about my health problems and were ready to work with them. They lived close to Barbara, and they assured me that Barbara's four children would be glad to care for her when I needed to go for doctor appointments.

I told them I would definitely consider it, and even though it hardly looked like my dream job, deep inside I knew that this was God's way of providing for me. It gave me a flexible source of income and a place to live, and perhaps I could even understand Barbara's suffering better than some people could have.

Saloma seemed to be as excited as I was about the amazing way God had answered my prayers that weekend. It seemed like a quick change of plans for me. The hardest part of it was knowing I would be so far from Saloma, who had become a close friend and confidant.

When I had my checkup with Dr. Ohler, I told him I was hoping to move back to Maryland. He gave his approval, saying that he and Dr. Howard could stay in touch and that I could always call him. Then he studied my face for a few moments and asked, "Don't you ever get depressed?"

I thought a little, then answered truthfully, "I definitely don't always feel happy-go-lucky, but I don't think I really do get depressed."

"Most people would get depressed with the pain and ongoing illness you've had to deal with. They become hopeless and see no reason for going on in life, then they start depending on antidepressants to cope. You seem to be coping." He shrugged. "Keep smiling."

I knew I would miss Virginia when I moved in September, but I also felt sure it was God who had orchestrated my circumstances. Sadie told me about two girls in Indiana who were looking for work, and she hired them over the phone. I truly was thrilled when I saw how God had met my needs, the girls' needs, and Sadie's needs. Seeing how He worked in the past gave me courage to move toward the future even though this new job brought some uncertainty. I was certain I would get along well with Chad's family and with Barbara, but I knew it would be a challenge as I learned to understand Barbara's wordless language.

Those first few weeks with Barbara proved somewhat frustrating for both of us as I learned to adapt to her daily routine and began translating her grunts and excited gestures into meaningful communication. Eventually, time and familiarity took a lot of the guesswork out of our "conversation."

I quickly fell in love with Chad and Pauline's family. They frequently included me in whatever they were doing, always making me feel welcome as though I were a part of the family. Rodney, the oldest of the four children, was twelve. Ryan and Loren followed him, and Michelle was six years old. They often came down to the house to play games.

Since I enjoyed baking, I tried out lots of cookie recipes on the children. The minute they came in the door, they headed for the cookie jar. "Any cookies today?" Of course, I loved every bit of it! The boys, especially, were rambunctious, teasing live wires, and they teased their poor sister Shellie mercilessly. Once in a while they also got me into trouble, like the time Loren started playing with the phone. Suddenly it started ringing, and I answered, "Hello?"

"Hello. Are you all right? Do you need help?" a man's voice asked in a no-nonsense tone.

"No." I replied, rather confused.

"This is 911. Do you have a child in the house?"

"Yes, I do." I answered.

"Will you make sure this does not happen again? I should be giving you a fine, but this time I'll just give you a warning." I never knew what those ornery youngsters would get into next!

One morning I got the urge to make doughnuts for Barbara's family who planned to get together that evening. I called Pauline and told her I'd love to stir up a batch of doughnuts if some of the children would like to come down and knead the dough since work like that aggravated the pain in my hands.

"Wait a minute and I'll ask the children."

"Yeah!" I heard enthusiastic yells in the background.

Soon the door flew open, and Loren and Michelle came running in. They washed their hands and thrust them into the dough, punching and kneading and pulling until it felt smooth and elastic. While we waited for the doughnuts to rise, we played Dutch Blitz, now a popular card game at my house. Loren nearly always won the game even though Michelle and I tried hard to give him a run for his money. The doughnuts soon disappeared, but the memories were mine to keep.

"Arlene, we reserved a beach house in Delaware for a weekend. Why don't you join us? We can surely find someone to take care of Barbara." That weekend was quickly added to my storehouse of precious memories, and it was full of laughter and love, though the love appeared in some smelly ways.

"Look out, Arlene," Loren yelled, dangling a horseshoe crab by its tail right under my nose.

"Gross!" Get that stinking thing out of here, you little teaser!"

Michelle also got her share of love from her brothers, though I think the poor dear sometimes wished they would just leave her alone. And I wished my stomach tormentors would leave me alone.

Eight months after Dr. Ohler snipped the common bile duct, some of the pancreas-related symptoms began appearing again. I had also been experiencing stiff, painful joints and muscles for quite some time, and when I finally went to see a chiropractor, he recommended that I meet with Dr. Mantel in Pittsburgh, which was more than a two-hour drive away. The chiropractor described Dr. Mantel as a medical doctor who had worked to combine modern methods with more natural methods focusing on nutrition and herbal remedies. Sometimes I felt like crying—I could not handle one more possible remedy; they never worked. But then I would bounce back and be ready to give the new idea a fair chance. Now, I felt ready to fall apart. How could I keep going on like this? I found I could face life only by taking one day at a time.

Dr. Mantel's diagnosis was clear: "You have a severe case of Chronic Fatigue Syndrome, an illness that is often misunderstood as a primarily psychological problem. People suffering from this malady are often accused of imagining their illness, and doctors say it is impossible for a person to have so many things wrong at the same time. I've researched it, and the medical field is now recognizing it as a serious medical problem. It probably showed up because your immune system is depleted and lacks the essential vitamins, making you susceptible to allergies."

I hardly knew whether or not to believe him. He immediately put me on a strict diet with vitamin supplements to build up my immune system. "Once your immune system builds up again, you'll feel like a different person," he promised. It had given me one more hope to cling to.

Sometimes, however, hope seemed like a flimsy thread. When I heard a group of my unmarried friends were planning a tour to Europe, feelings of loneliness and jealousy swept over me. My health did not allow me to go to places I would so much have liked to visit, and, of course, my health care took all but the money I needed for the bare necessities. How could I be happy for them when life felt so unfair? Marriage was hardly an option for me as my health left me with barely anything but life itself. Neither did I have the independence and ability to do things that happy singles could do. I did not fit into any group of people, and wasn't that sense of belonging something everyone needed for happiness?

I still remember the year I was in third grade as one of the most painful times of my life. I knew I did not feel well, but my friends could not understand why. Neither could I. The other girls nagged, "Come on, Arlene, why do you always sit back here under the tree like a bump on a log? If we have to go out to the ball diamond, you have to, too."

I swallowed the big lump in my throat. "I can't. It makes my chest hurt, and my heart pounds like crazy," I tried to explain, commanding my tears to stay away. Did they think I liked sitting alone, watching them play? They just didn't understand. I had never felt so alone in my life, and my friends were turning on me when I most needed them. I came home from school and cried to Mom. Although she had little to say, her presence made all the difference in the world. My schoolmates eventually adjusted to my handicaps, but I never forgot that forsaken feeling. A few decades later, I still sometimes felt that others have gone on with their lives and left me alone. This time, I cried to my heavenly Parent. He had little to say, but His presence made all the difference in the world.

After the blood work results came back to Dr. Mantel, he explained them to me. "Believe it or not, you are also allergic to yourself. Your cells are fighting against you instead of for you." I felt that happening internally too, and I fought the feelings of envy and despair. I didn't need my spirit and soul becoming as messed up as my body!

I knew I had many allergy problems over the years. One of the first times it showed up, I was still in elementary school. For an art project, the older students had glued pasta of many shapes, sizes, and colors onto a piece of plywood to make a peacock. They then sprayed shellac over the finished product for protection. I thought the peacock was beautiful, but it was not long before I started getting sick from the smell. The results of the allergic reaction kept me home from school for a week. After that experience, I often became very ill whenever I even smelled paint. In recent years, however, the paint smell does not give me a reaction.

When I reacted to some of the prescribed supplements Dr. Mantel was giving me, he recommended IV therapy twice a week to bolster my immune system as well as detailed allergy testing. Often when the time came for IV injections, the nurses spent two or three hours trying to find my veins. They tried soaking my arms and hands in hot water and even tried soaking my feet with the intention of finding a vein there. If that did not work, they moved to the artery in my neck. And too often, they finally gave up. These sessions with the needle were not my idea of fun. With five hours of driving added to the therapy time, the days seemed to stretch out unbearably long.

I was not well enough to make these trips alone, but I detested needing to ask others to drive to Pittsburgh. How could I repay them? How could my life be worth more than all the trouble it was causing? This neediness has been one of the most difficult parts of my life, in some ways a more bitter pill than the pain itself. Eventually, I was going to treatment three times a week. The long days exhausted me, and I could not see how that would help me in the long run because of the physical exhaustion they induced. Finally, we decided to make reservations in a motel close to Dr. Mantel's office.

Over the years, it had become impossible to handle all my medical bills without insurance, but by then no sensible health insurance company would accept a client with my history. Individuals gave generously, and different groups did fund-raisers to help with my expenses. The hospitals knocked most of their bills to a fraction of the normal amount, but the pressure on the church and our family continued until I applied for federal disability funding, which proved to be a lifesaver, literally. Nevertheless, since I was still unable to work regularly, and the traveling costs and other related expenses continued, I cannot say I never worried again. The cost of Dr. Mantel's program and my meager finances were on my mind when I got an interesting phone call.

"Hello, Ms. Kauffman, how are you today?" asked a man's voice.

"Pretty good, thank you." It was an answer I gave without thinking, and I was quite certain he would not want to know half of the truth.

"I am calling concerning your health insurance. What are you paying?" he asked.

I explained that our church operated a "sharing fund" to which people gave voluntarily as they were able to do so, and then a certain percentage of all medical bills were paid out of that fund.

"I never heard anything like that," he said. "Does it work?"

"Yes, it does. We want to support each other emotionally and spiritually as well as financially, and this has a way of bringing us together," I tried to explain. "Sometimes we need to do fund-raisers. And in some cases, we do use insurance."

"But don't you want to help your church save money? How old are you? Are you in good health?"

After I briefly explained my medical condition, he quickly said, "I'm sorry, you won't be eligible for insurance. How about starting a burial fund? Do you know how much it costs to bury somebody today?" He must have been desperate, but I was not ready yet to crawl into my coffin.

My Aunt Darlene, diagnosed with multiple sclerosis, also started treatments in Pittsburgh, and we drove those long miles together. Darlene came from a family of nineteen and could tell story after story about those years. She and Barbara, another "doctor's office friend," hit it off, and Barbara invited us to stay with her and her husband Roy rather than paying so much for motel rooms. Barbara was a delightfully entertaining, gregarious Christian who proudly introduced herself as "Barbara Fisher, a happy Methodist."

At the end of the day in the doctor's office, Barbara and Darlene often headed for the swimming pool in the backyard while I dragged myself upstairs and collapsed on the bed. No matter how much I rested, I could not build up my reservoir of energy. After dinner, Barbara and Darlene laughed and gabbed and played the piano late into the night, but I again headed for my bed, alone and grieving for the youth that I felt I never had.

Chapter 14

"Is any one of you sick? He should call the elders of the church to pray over him and anoint him with oil in the name of the Lord. And the prayer offered in faith will make the sick person well; the Lord will raise him up. If he has sinned, he will be forgiven. Therefore confess your sins to each other and pray for each other so that you may be healed. The prayer of a righteous man is powerful and effective" (James 5:14-16, NIV).

Certainly, those words in the book of James held a message for me. I wanted to step out in faith, asking God to work a miracle. The ministerial team at my church was happy to meet to join me in prayer, petitioning the Great Healer to show us His power and His love. The anointing with oil represented a special setting apart—I was sanctified, made holy and consecrated—for whatever God wanted to accomplish in my life. If that meant giving me a healthy body, we would forever rejoice.

To think or talk about suffering is one thing; to suffer is another. Often those who have never been there have all the answers, like Job's friends, whom he called "miserable comforters." Some people insinuated that my illness resulted from some hidden sin or lack of faith. Like Jesus' disciples, they assumed that the person who suffers deserves their affliction for some reason.

"As he [Jesus] went along, he saw a man blind from birth. His disciples asked Him, 'Rabbi, who sinned, this man or his parents, that he was born blind?' 'Neither this man nor his parents sinned,' said Jesus, 'but this happened so that the work of God might be displayed in his life' " (John 9:1-3, NIV). When Jesus' own friend, Lazarus, became ill, Jesus said, "This sickness will not end in death. No, it is for God's glory so that God's Son may be glorified through it" (John 11:4, NIV).

This beautiful time together still holds a sacred place in my heart as I remember and relive the personal cleansing and renewal that came as I honestly told God that I badly wanted to be healed, but I wanted even more for His plan to be accomplished. I prayed once again that God would show me any unknown sin in my life, knowing that harboring wrong attitudes or actions in my heart would definitely have physical and emotional as well as spiritual consequences.

A Cry From a Tent Dweller

It was nice living in this tent when it was strong and secure, and when the sun was shining and the air was warm. But, Mr. Tentmaker, it is so scary now. My tent is acting like it is not going to hold together. The poles seem weak, and they shift with the wind. A few stakes have wiggled loose from the sand, and worst of all, the canvas has a rip. It no longer protects me from beating rain or stinging flies.

It's scary in here, Mr. Tentmaker. Last week I was sent to the repair shop, and some repairman tried to patch the rip in my canvas. It didn't help much, though, because the patch pulled away from the edges, and now the tear is worse. What troubles me the most, Mr. Tentmaker, is that the repairman didn't seem to notice I was still in the tent. He just worked on the canvas while I shivered inside. I cried out once but no one heard me.

I guess my first real question is, *Why did you make me such a flimsy tent?* I can see by looking around the campground that some of the other tents are much stronger and more stable. Why, Mr. Tentmaker, did you pick a tent of such poor quality for me, and even more importantly, what do you intend to do about it?

An Answer From the Tentmaker

Oh, little tent dweller, as the Creator and Provider of tents, I know about you and your tent, and I love you both.

I once made a tent for myself and lived in it on your campground. My tent was vulnerable, too, and some vicious attackers ripped it to pieces while I was still in it. It was a terrible experience, but you will be glad to know they couldn't hurt me. In fact, the whole occurrence brought a tremendous advantage because it is this very victory over my enemy that frees me to be of present help to you.

Little tent dweller, I am now prepared to come and live in your tent with you, if you will invite me. We will dwell together, and you will find that real security comes from my being in your tent with you. When the storms come, you can huddle in my arms, and I'll hold you. When the canvas rips, we'll go to the repair shop together.

Someday, little tent dweller, your tent will collapse, for I've only designed it for temporary use. When that time comes, you and I will leave together. I promise not to leave before you. Then, free of all that would hinder or restrict, we will move to our permanent home and together rejoice and be glad—forever (anonymous, adapted).

A young girl once asked me, "Isn't it selfish to want to die just to get away from suffering and pain?" It seems to me that God would be saddened if we did not long to be freed from this sin-trampled world which groans like a woman giving birth. Like Apostle Paul describes, we "groan inwardly as we wait eagerly for our adoption as sons, the redemption of our bodies" (Romans 8:23, NIV). Jesus Himself wept after Lazarus' death even though He knew that the ending of the story would be happy. Honesty with God and myself about both my positive and negative feelings has brought beautiful freedom. After all, the preface to those verses in James acknowledges our feelings: "Is any one of you in trouble? He should pray. Is anyone happy? Let him sing songs of praise. Is any one of you sick? He should call the elders of the church" (James 5:13, NIV). Jesus also wept and felt deeply. I for one can hardly wait to claim the new body and the mansions my Lord has promised me. Even so come quickly, Lord Jesus.

Chapter 15

I was pleased with the improvements that came with the treatment of my allergies, but in July I was admitted to the hospital with pancreatitis for the third time in four months. Dr. Howard sent me to see Dr. Ohler, who confirmed my fears. Scar tissue was restricting the bile flow, and they needed to cut the sphincter again. How could I willingly resign myself to getting pancreatitis? Although the word was becoming entirely too common in my vocabulary, the pain was like the very first time I got it. "I'll eat my hat if you get pancreatitis," Dr. Ohler declared. "I'll go in, make a snip, and be right back out." I had heard all this before. Why did they bother trying to make false promises?

On my twenty-fifth birthday, I went in for my fourth ERCP. They were ready to put the scope down my throat when I begged them to wait until I was asleep, but they went ahead as though I didn't exist.

Dr. Ohler apologized afterwards. "The problem is that we can't completely put you to sleep until you swallow the tube, and for some reason after that you were still with us. We give our patients something in the IV line so they do not remember the procedure, but I know you did. Like I expected, the common bile duct had blocked the flow, so it should go better again as long as it lasts."

"Dr. Ohler, get out your hat and eat it! I have pancreatitis starting." But he said not a word. What could he say? I lived through another nightmare with pain for the next two weeks.

I recovered from that bout and then went for a "vegetable soup test." I ate the dye-injected soup so we could see how quickly food moved through my digestive system. It took my stomach three times longer to empty than it should have, which explained the reason for my discomfort. My doctor wanted to start me on a drug brought in from Canada. It cost $300 a month and was not yet FDA approved, but Dr. Ohler convinced me of its effectiveness in speeding up the digestive processes and offered to have it mailed directly to my home. During one of my appointments with Dr. Howard, he asked me if the drug was legal. "If you're jailed in Canada for smuggling drugs across the border, be sure to tell them you need a doctor to go along; I want to go fishing."

Barbara's family showed such graciousness in spite of my complete lack of dependability that I knew for certain that God had brought me to this job. I made many trips between Maryland and Virginia, sometimes staying in Virginia for up to three weeks at a time for doctor visits and tests and the resulting pancreatitis attacks. I felt like a nuisance and bother to everyone—bumming off of kind Saloma and her family in Virginia, regularly running out on my job in Maryland, and confusing the already-frustrated doctors at both places.

I had some tests scheduled in Maryland when a good old Garrett County blizzard showed up. My sister Miriam and I braved the weather and made is over Mount Savage, at last descending into the milder weather east of the mountains. As the anesthesia wore off after the test, I reentered the storm. My blood pressure soared and I started gasping for air. Miriam rushed off to find a nurse. "Looks like an allergic reaction," she said with a grimace. "Let me call the doctor."

A very irritable doctor entered the room. "I don't understand it. There is no reason for this. It's time for you to get out of here," he snapped.

The nurses stood up for me and held their own. "This girl is sick and in absolutely no shape to go home! If you don't do something for her, we will and you're out of the picture." He reluctantly had me admitted to the hospital, and the nurses did all they could to make both me and Miriam comfortable, even finding a private room for Miriam to spend the night.

In the morning when the doctor made his rounds, he was still upset. "There's no reason you should have to be hospitalized," he said crisply. "I'm glad I don't have to take care of you again." By that time, the feeling was mutual. A much friendlier doctor took his place, and a week later I returned home with a generally positive test report. The tumor still showed pre-cancerous cells similar to what had been found the autumn before, but they did not seem to be of huge concern to anyone, so I did not worry about them, either.

It had now been a year since the last time I had been hospitalized with pancreatitis, but the constant pain and nausea continued at least in part because the sphincter kept closing up. Dr. Howard sent me to see Dr. Ohler again. Dr. Ohler had reached the end of his resources and asked if I would consider going to North Union to see Dr. Ball, his colleague at Southeast University Hospital, one of the Nation's leaders in research and technology. What else could I do? I could hardly turn away from the possibility of finding one who could actually help me. They warned me that he would be doing more tests, so I needed to be prepared to stay for a couple days. "Hopefully, you can be back home in time for Christmas," Dr. Ohler said. "You've got seven days." His sheepish grin told me he knew better.

To help cover the costs for gas, motel, and food, we made and sold sub-like sandwiches, what we in Pennsylvania call hoagies. We formed two assembly lines to place cold cuts, lettuce, tomatoes, pickles and onions on the hoagie roll, and we sold more than a thousand hoagies by noon. Many people gave more than the hoagies cost, and when we counted up the proceeds, I felt completely overwhelmed with thankfulness, less for the money than for the priceless gift of knowing that people cared about me.

The Sunday before Mom, Miriam, and I headed south toward Sue University Hospital, my church had a special prayer for me, asking God to give me peace and courage. The night was cold and starry as we drove toward the city, which was lit up with Christmas lights. I expected to face another incident of pancreatitis, but I felt such a calm restfulness that could have come only because of all the prayers my friends were sending up for me.

The hospital was so enormous that they sent me from one section of the hospital to another in an ambulance. Maybe Dr. Ball, a tall man with gray hair, would pull a rabbit out of a hat and give me some answers. He looked like a wise sort of man, I thought. He ran me through the gauntlet of tests the first day and did an ERCP the second day. After the procedure, I started to wake up. I could hardly believe it! I had been asleep! Dr. Ball, however, could not save me from the inevitable pancreatitis.

One quiet afternoon while Mom and Miriam were sitting with me, I saw Mom look out into the hallway and smile.

"Mom, what do you see?"

"You're getting visitors!" My brother Alton and an aunt and uncle who lived in North Carolina stopped by. Their familiar faces brought such joy to me. Spending the holiday season in the hospital hardly thrilled me, but I felt a sense of purpose in even this unfortunate timing. It seems few people actually experience the peace and joy that ought to characterize Christmas time. I knew that if others could witness my positive response to spending Christmas stuck in a hospital bed, they could recognize the marks of a miracle-working Christ living in me. In fact, my whole hospital stay seemed strangely quiet—we had received no cards, no phone calls, no flowers. Mom finally went to investigate, and the receptionist told her, "We have no Arlene Kauffman in the hospital."

When Mom told her I had been there for ten days, the lady apologized profusely. The mail had been returned or tossed into the trash can, the flowers and phone calls not accepted.

On Christmas morning, an enormous poinsettia arrived and lent a Christmas aura to my hospital room, and several people from home called to carol and wish me a happy Christmas. Christmas Day at Southeast University was a quiet one except for some men who caroled in the halls and stopped at my door when they saw my delight. My generous aunt drove two hours to bring a full-course Christmas dinner for Mom and Miriam. It sure beat cafeteria food!

On December 29, Dr. Ball stopped by again and told me he had no suggestions for me that Dr. Ohler had not already tried. If we saw no improvement, he recommended we consider placing a stent in the duct to keep it open.

Chapter 16

I clearly remember the chill of that dreary February afternoon when Mom called and said only, "Can you come up to James' house? I need to talk to you." The quiet, defeated tone of her voice told me something had happened, and my first hunch proved to be true: Dad had asked Mom to leave the house. My legs shook and my heart pulsed with pain, both for myself and for Mom. I stopped in to talk briefly to Pauline, whose hug and quick prayer helped calm my soul.

"What can we do now? Where can we go? Was he serious? Does he realize what this means for him?" My four youngest siblings, now in their teens and lower twenties, voluntarily chose to go with Mom when she left because they knew what we all knew: she had suffered alone for years while giving herself and her strength to create a safe place for our hearts. Now she needed us.

Martha's sensitive spirit tore her into pieces. "I can't leave Dad alone at the house! Can't we just go back? Who will take care of him? He'll be so lonely." We had God and each other, but Dad struggled alone.

Knowing instinctively that behind his silence lived a miserable man, we had long been sending prayers and tears heavenward, begging God to release our father from his bitterness and loneliness. But Dad needed to make that decision, and over the past twenty years, he had been making some negative choices. In the early years of their marriage, Mom knew him as a loving husband and father, and his neighbors knew him as one of the most genial, generous men around. The changes that brought on his unpredictable outbursts of anger had been gradual, and they now had brought him to this. It seemed our sorrow would bury us alive as we grieved for both our own loss—the years without an emotionally present father—and his loss.

Mom wanted to go back home to the farm in the evening and pretend nothing had happened, but she finally decided to follow the advice of others to leave rather than placing herself in a potentially volatile situation. While our brothers and sisters from church were asking God to provide safety and wisdom to us, Mom and my siblings did return to the house to gather some of their belongings, and Mom prepared Dad's favorite meal: hamburgers, macaroni and cheese, corn, and, of course, applesauce loaded with sugar. We had often joked that Dad ate cereal with his sugar instead of sugar with his cereal. Now none of them felt like eating, but Dad sat down at the table and attacked his food with such a hearty appetite that they wondered if he had meant what he said. Had it just been a storm that came and went?

After eating together, they washed the dishes and cleaned the house, then they loaded up some of their belongings and camped out in James and Joanna's home. Immediately, our church family lavished us with food as a way of communicating their care and concern for our pain. We certainly did not feel like cooking or even eating. People from church called and asked, "What can we do for you?" Their kindness meant so much, but we were all in a daze and did not know ourselves what we needed. We greatly benefited from those who just saw needs and met them, but perhaps it was Jeffery, my charming eight-month-old nephew, who brought the most healing to us while we waited for the shock to wear off.

Now, as in my sickness, I learned about ways to show love. Many people feel uncomfortable because they don't know what to say, but the fact is, we would not remember any eloquent speeches anyway. "I love you," "I'm sorry," or "I'm praying" all work to show the love of God, as do hugs, flowers, cards, or sometimes just giving those who are hurting a chance to talk without judging them.

That first month wearied us all. Would Dad change his mind? He would not tell us what he was thinking. Should we rent a home temporarily or build? We just wished we could stop the world and get off, but life went on.

God gave Mom a verse from Isaiah 41 that helped her through this difficult time. "Do not fear, for I am with you, be not dismayed for I am your God. I will strengthen you and I will help you" (Isaiah 41:10, NIV). While we sat around the table trying to decide what to do, David voiced our plea: "Oh, Dad, why did you have to make life so hard?"

After we decided to buy a lot and build, more love poured in as people donated labor, groceries, money, and gifts. In two months, we moved into the house. My siblings had taken most of their belongings, but Mom had picked up only her clothes and her quilt frame, hoping to return soon. In the months following the move, I learned to know a mother I had not known before. She had been kept subdued for so many years, and now she surprised me with her strength, humor, and liveliness.

My mother's response to Dad gave us an enormous amount of respect for her. She always showed love in spite of his faults, and her sincere faithfulness to the man she had married still stands as a shining witness to the kind of forgiveness Jesus taught. My father subjected her to tremendous emotional pain; this she never denied. Nor did she pretend that everything was all right. But she still holds onto the memories of what he once was and what she believes he still could be. Ultimately, she chose mercy and pity rather than anger and resentment, and we had grown up learning from her. Her life stands as living proof that love is stronger than pain.

"Why didn't you leave or become bitter?" Mom asked Danny one day after he was married with a family of his own.

"Mom," he said, "if you would have hated Dad for the way he treated us, I never would have become a Christian. I couldn't have believed in God's love if I hadn't seen it in you." Mom wept tears of thankfulness. She had had no idea of how strong or how lasting would be the influence of her life.

All this happened in February 1992, and at the time I am writing this in 2007, it has been seven years since we were last able to contact Dad. Even though things weren't the way they should have been, Mom and all seven of us children still grieve for him, and we would all invite him back with wide-open arms. Mom often reminds us that he was not always that way. He played ball with his sons and declared that if anyone would try to hurt his girls, they would forever regret it. In his heart, he loved us. We hold onto that knowledge now, after our own pain and remembrance of his outbursts sometimes cloud what we believe really was in his heart.

Chapter 17

I spent as much time with Barbara that spring as I could, but hospital visits continued. No other job would have been as flexible, and few other families would have shown the patience that Barbara's family showed. Smooth muscle syndrome continued to cause trouble, as the muscles of my digestive system became ineffective for transporting food. Dr. Ohler told me the disorder could affect any part of the body, and apparently nearly my entire body was affected, possibly explaining the pain in my hands. My appointment with a specialist brought new possible diagnoses, including multiple sclerosis and lupus, but it was still in the early stages. The pain in my hands and feet lessened over the years, although the doctors wondered if the increased pain medication I had been taking merely covered up the pain. Because of continued battles with urinary tract infections, I was put on an antibiotic indefinitely.

When Martha and our cousin Susie drove down to Virginia to pick me up after more tests with Dr. Ohler, they did Saloma's housecleaning. That dear woman had done so much for me that I knew I could never repay her. During the times I was in great pain, whether day or night, I frequently went to the sewing machine and pieced wall hangers or pot holders. Saloma could always pick up on how I was feeling by the sound of the machine; the worse I hurt, the harder I pushed the foot control.

Dr. Ohler wanted to do another ERCP to check the status of the common bile duct. Three days before the scheduled ERCP I felt another pancreatic attack coming on, so I called Dr. Ohler.

"It can't possibly be pancreatitis. You had no ERCP done, so I don't know what it could be." He sent me to the local hospital emergency room. Another arrival, an unresponsive heart attack victim, had priority. As I sat waiting for what seemed like forever, the tears streamed down my face because of the pain, and I felt that Dr. Ohler had somehow let me down. Couldn't he trust me even now to know what pain was "real pain"? When the blood work results came back, the doctor walked in with disbelief on his face and said, "The pancreas numbers shown on the results cannot possibly be correct—they're higher than any on record!" He sent me to Charles Town while he repeated the blood work tests, but he did give me a light dose of morphine to ease the pain a little bit.

"Should we go by ambulance?" Saloma asked.

"You're just wasting time by waiting on the ambulance! Get going now!" he insisted.

I did not know how much longer I could handle the pain. Turning my head to the side, I shut my eyes and just let the tears roll down my cheeks. I felt every bump on the road. We finally arrived in the emergency room, and I let Saloma speak for me.

The ER doctor called Little Rock for the blood work reports, then called Saloma to the desk and told her that my numbers had broken the record. "I'm going to increase her morphine so she can get some rest. It's the worst case of pancreatitis I ever saw; this is really serious." Although this was in the middle of the night, he called the doctor who was covering Dr. Ohler to come in to see me.

Saloma, her eyes wet with helpless tears, stayed with me until the morphine made the pain more nearly tolerable. The next morning Saloma called the hospital to see how my night went.

"She is in surgery now," the nurse reported.

Saloma was shocked and upset. "I'm the contact person. Why wasn't I notified?" She immediately called Mom and told her I was in surgery.

"But she can't be! I just talked to her," responded Mom.

The nurse had gotten names and people mixed up, but by this time I felt ready for surgery. Why not get rid of that horrid pancreas?

I could not imagine my situation getting worse. One of our pastors drove Mom to Charles Town, and when she walked in the door, all I could do was cry. "Mom, it hurts so bad."

Dr. Ohler stopped in to see me on his way home from church. He looked distressed to see me crying while Mom sat beside me, stroking my arm. He knew I could handle incredible pain without tears.

"Dr. Ohler, please do something for this pain!"

He pulled on his necktie. "Arlene," he said in a quiet voice, "I'll do my best, no matter what it takes, to get you relief. I just don't understand what is happening." He stood there by my bed until I relaxed and seemed to be resting.

We heard him asking the nursing staff, as he went out the door, "Who's the surgeon on call?"

Did that mean he considered doing an emergency surgery? He kept a close watch on me all day, even though it was his day off, and tried to keep me as comfortable as possible. His care warmed my heart, and I never forgot his kindness. It took me ten days to recover, but every single time that I start feeling better, I just feel so grateful to have that excruciating pain gone.

During one of my hospital stays, Chad and Pauline came for a visit and also told me that they wanted to release me from feeling that I needed to get back to care for Barbara. Chads soon moved in with Barbara, and never once did they make me feel guilty for what I could not do. I had not been home long when Mary Jane called and renewed her offer to let me work at her shop whenever I liked.

It was comforting to have a backup plan for work because I now had chronic pancreatitis that cropped up without warning. Pain ruled my life and had become, strangely, part of my identity, part of who I was. I could not understand why I needed to suffer like this, and I probably would not understand even if God told me. Like Paul asked three times to have his "thorn in the flesh" removed, I prayed for healing. God did not perform the miracle Paul hoped for, but God did perform a different kind of a miracle when He gave the Apostle Paul strength in the midst of his weakness. I also claimed the promise

God made: "My grace is sufficient for thee, for my strength is made perfect in weakness." Like Paul, I also say, "Most gladly, therefore, will I rather glory in my infirmities that the power of Christ may rest upon me . . . for when I am weak then am I strong" (2 Corinthians 12:9, 10). Those who have never experienced deep trials will never know the satisfying peace that comes from total surrender while experiencing difficulties. Even so, I would never wish half of my pain on my worst enemy.

In the summer of 1993, our family rented a cabin in the mountains of West Virginia. The year had been difficult in many ways, and Mom felt we needed some fun time together again as a way of healing. We had set up a bake stand during the Spring Folk Festival in October the year before and earned the money we needed for our vacation.

With Mom, her seven children, two grandchildren, one in-law, Martha's boyfriend, and Danny's girlfriend all packed into a cabin, we made quite a jolly uproar, though we also shared some serious times. The weekend held lots of fun, including boating, table games, visiting Blackwater Falls, and driving through the park at dusk where hundreds of deer appeared, some sticking their heads in the car windows for the apple we offered.

After lunch was prepared and served on the deck, the women of the family struck upon the brilliant idea that the two dating couples should do the dishes and put away the food. All but four people cheered, and the two guys made faces. But what choice did they have, since they had the girls to impress?

"Okay, who dumped the water on Andrew?" Martha yelled. A battle was in the air. Regardless of who actually started it, Miriam probably deserves the blame just because of all the times she survived unscathed after her pranks. Soon everyone was involved, and even Mom and I got wet though we were innocent bystanders. The fun continued until after dark, and we will never let Martha forget how she met up with the stone wall at the cabin. After everyone knew she had only scraped her nose and needed a Band-Aid, she endured more than her fair share of teasing!

As the vacation time ended, I felt packed full of new memories and happiness, and I felt so grateful I could spend this time with my family between doctors' visits and pancreatitis attacks. It had really been a wonderful time, although we all were aware that the family circle had not been complete: Dad had not been there.

Dr. Ohler decided to try placing a stent in the common bile duct to keep it open, like Dr. Ball had suggested. Of course, pancreatitis flared up again from the procedure, but eventually I was back at my babysitting job. As my pain gradually increased, my excitement faded, but I refused to accept the fact that the stent was not going to work. When I saw Dr. Ohler, he sent me to the hospital for a quick X-ray to see where the stent was and if it could be causing the irritation. The technician had a difficult time seeing what he was supposed to be seeing and called Dr. Ohler.

"I'll be right up to take a look," Dr. Ohler told him.

When the X-ray room door opened, the defeated look on Dr. Ohler's face said too much. "I'm sorry, but the stent is gone."

I did not dare let myself cry. I thought if I started, I would never stop. *God, I'm human. How much do you expect me to take?* How I wished the Lord would appear and simply say, "I am still in control." As I got back to Saloma's house, a vehicle followed me into the driveway. I stepped out, and the woman questioned, "Kauffman?" Someone had sent me a gorgeous flower arrangement, and I knew it was God's way of telling me, "I'm here."

Chapter 18

My family was working hard in November of 1993, frantically preparing for Andrew and Martha's wedding. We were expecting 400 guests. Martha had asked me to be a bridesmaid, and I was feeling worse and worse. Surely I could make it to my sister's wedding!

Just three days before the wedding, a social worker called and said, "I'm bringing you an eight-month-old boy. His name is John. Mom and Miriam had taken classes to enroll in foster care a year before and now, suddenly, they were sending us a child.

"Today?" Mom asked.

"Yes, as soon as I can get there. I have him with me now. We don't really know anything about him, except that he's in need of a good home. His mother is in foster care herself."

Blond-headed John adjusted very well and seemed to be the most cheery boy around. He absolutely loved Danny and David, squealing with delight when he saw them coming.

Mom knew that because family and friends would be swarming our house, a quiet place to rest would be hard to come by. With her typical thoughtfulness, she called my aunt Mary and asked her if she had a spare bed for me so I could avoid the commotion of wedding preparations at home. She and Uncle Eli were closely involved with a mission in Honduras, where Eli was at the time of the wedding. Softhearted Mary treated me like a queen and, in a typical expression of her gracious spirit, insisted on moving upstairs so I could sleep in the master bedroom. After my family left the farm, Mary periodically took Dad a pie, and he seemed to appreciate her quiet gesture of love. I had no way of knowing that this week would be the last time we would see Mary. She joined Eli in Honduras and both were killed tragically when the bus they were driving lost its brakes. Their story and the heart-wrenching account of their family's experiences are told in an aptly titled book, *Triumphant Over Tragedy.*

On the day of the wedding, I so badly wanted to avoid being a bother, but I felt awful. Secretly, I wondered if there was any way I could make it through the day. I experienced the wedding and reception in a daze, determined to last through my sister's special day.

"Arlene, you look sick," Mom said as she and Saloma tried to persuade me to go to the emergency room.

"I'll be okay. I don't want to go, and everyone is busy. Besides, who would take me?" Earl appeared at my shoulder. "Come on, Arlene, I'll take you to the ER and stay with you till your mom can get away."

Dr. Howard pumped me full of fluids and kept me overnight with an order to head to Virginia as soon as possible. In Virginia, Dr. Ohler made a proposal. "You're probably about ready to throw me out, but what do you think about placing a bigger stent? Hopefully, a bigger one will stay where it belongs."

I reluctantly agreed. Another ERCP and pancreatitis put me back in the hospital. Before I was discharged, my pain again worsened, so they took another X-ray and found that the stent was already dislodged. Dr. Ohler was keeping surgery only as a backup if all else failed. All else was quickly failing, but he wanted to do yet another ERCP to stitch the stent in place.

"I don't know who is the most frustrated, you or me. But give me your pen," I sighed. "I'll sign the consent form. But can't you find a way to put me to sleep? And with all this pancreatitis, I've had enough pain to have had fifty babies."

The ERCP kept me in the hospital during the holiday season, and one morning while I was wishing I could go home, I heard a commotion coming from across the hall. The nurse was putting restraints on a man who had attempted suicide. "Listen," she said, "we're trying to help you."

After he stopped fighting, I heard him sobbing, and later, "It's

Christmas, and I don't have anybody who will ever miss me. I just want to end it all." At that moment, I felt so small. I was surrounded with people who loved me, who wished I could be with them, who would have done anything to see me get well. How could I complain when God had given me the most precious gifts? When some of my family drove five hours to be with me and help me celebrate Christmas, I struggled with feelings of guilt. The world is not fair.

In late January, a snowstorm blew into Virginia, and although Maryland folks might not have been fazed by this bit of snow blowing about, Virginia folks holed up in their homes for the day. I sure hoped my pain would stay under control, but it threatened to erupt into full-blown pancreatitis.

Earl stayed home from work, so Saloma popped corn and pulled out the Rumicube game, and we played for hours. Finally, I could ignore the increasing pain no longer. This time Katie, a generous lady from next door, and Earl drove through the winter wonderland to Charles Town. While we waited in the ER as usual, Katie related a story of a man who had come into the ER with hemorrhoids. He wearied of waiting, so he threw himself on the floor and began kicking and screaming. That brought him the attention he wanted, and he was taken back to an examination room.

"What do you think, Katie? Should I try it? I hurt with something worse than hemorrhoids!" I threatened with a lopsided grin. In spite of my pain, I wondered what Dr. Ohler would do if I convinced him I had "lost it."

Dr. Ohler decided because of the irritation the stent caused to send me back to Southeast University to let Dr. Ball remove the stent Dr. Ohler had stitched in. While I was at Southeast University, a new doctor came in, looking over my medical history and asking lots of questions. He finally said, "I'd like to do some unusual tests. You are, after all, an unusual case, and there's just got to be help out there for you."

That was fine with me. After the results came back, another doctor paid me a visit and, obviously expecting an affirmative answer, asked if I had ever had a blood transfusion. I replied that I had not.

"Are you sure you never had a transfusion?" he questioned me the second time.

"I'm sure."

Looking at Mom, he asked, "Did she ever have a blood transfusion?"

Mom also told him that I had not, and he left, apparently unsatisfied. What convinced them I had had a blood transfusion I wondered? The next time Dr. Ball was in, Mom asked him. He explained that one of my blood tests showed a foreign antibody such as is usually found in people who have had blood transfusions in which the donated blood was not properly matched with the patient's blood. "In some cases," he explained, "antibodies are formed that then attack any organ in the body. You have already had your thyroid removed, then your gallbladder, and now the pancreas and bladder are giving you problems while that smooth muscle syndrome messes up your whole digestive system."

If his theory is correct that I acquired a foreign antibody from an outside source, the only possible explanation we have found traces back to the immunization shots I got when I started school. Even this we have no way of proving.

"What can be done about it?" I asked.

"We could put you on cortisone or give you a total change of blood, but then you'll get into other complications. I don't recommend it. We're also at a standstill with your pancreas problem." Then he added, "But don't despair, Arlene. The medical world progresses rapidly, and perhaps at some point in time they'll find some answers for you."

Living in Maryland and driving to Virginia to see Dr. Ohler every time I experienced a setback finally became too much to deal with. I understood that Saloma simply could not do full justice to both me and her family. They had sacrificed time and so much more to help me, and the time had come to make some changes. I temporarily moved in with Mom and three of my siblings, although John and my nieces and nephews, all rambunctious youngsters, filled the house with more activity than people who deal with chronic illness might wish for.

I soon found a quiet, ground level basement apartment on the edge of town that proved to be perfectly suited to my needs. Emily, a nurse, lived alone upstairs, so that meant I would be alone—and not alone. I also began searching for a job I could do from home at my own erratic pace, and when an advertisement came for correspondence courses from At-Home Professions, I decided to take a course for medical transcription. Even though I became ill and never went on to get a job after I graduated, I truly enjoyed the course and found it quite helpful for understanding the medical jargon I encountered all the time.

If I wanted to stop traveling to Virginia to see Dr. Ohler, I needed to find another GI doctor. Dr. Ohler was no miracle worker, I had discovered, but few if any doctors matched his knowledge and expertise. After making it a matter of prayer, I called Western Maryland University Hospital and inquired about a GI doctor.

"Yes, we have a Dr. Nelson who could see you soon," they said.

In his office, I looked up when a tall man with dark hair and a generally unimpressed expression shuffled in and unceremoniously flopped himself down on the chair across from me. Making no eye contact and blowing bubbles with his gum, he said, "I'm Dr. Henry." Then he added almost as an afterthought, "What can I do for you today?" By all appearances, he was not at all interested in whatever I was about to say.

"I see no reason why you should have pancreatitis. You tell me you never drank. No other family members have pancreatitis. I can't give you anything for pain without evidence of a problem. I can do an ERCP if you would like, but I'm sure I won't find a thing. Why don't you go home for now, and if you need something, call me back." Clearly, this option did not look promising. I heard later that he is known for being difficult to work with, and I had no trouble believing that!

When I told my housemate Emily about my dilemma, she offered to check in with a friend who works in Grant Town as a nurse to see if she could recommend another GI doctor. When I saw Dr. Rifes, I knew he was a gift from God.

"I'm thinking you have scar tissue closing the ducts again, so that's what we need to find out. My nurse will get you set up for another ERCP." He said it so easily—"let's do another ERCP." Just because I had endured so many in no way made me immune to the pain during and after the procedure. He promised to do his best to keep me comfortable and, as usual, I hoped this one would be better than any of the others. I have had a total of fourteen ERCPs performed in my life, and all I can say is that had I known after that first time how often they would stick that scope down my throat, I could never have made it.

Chapter 19

Sunday mornings were quiet, and my thoughts nearly always turned toward what would be happening in church. Remembering it as a time of encouragement, fellowship, and learning more about God, I felt alone and left out now that I was stuck at home and could not take part in church life. Therefore, I was overjoyed and very thankful when they started a visitation program so that every Sunday morning a family from church would have the chance to spend a short time of worship with me or with others whose health did not allow them to attend church regularly.

Lorraine, my good friend who often stopped to see me on her way home from work at Goodwill Nursing Home on Sunday afternoons, told me about the tradition of renting a cabin in Canaan Valley for a weekend that the single girls from their church kept every summer. She said they would be happy if I could join them. I was so touched and excited by Lorraine's thoughtfulness and told her that they were mighty brave to invite me. Wherever I go, if I will be gone more than a day, I take with me boxes of IV pumps and poles, tubes, syringes, flushes, and more. I anticipated the weekend with pleasure. With some help, I finally got all my medical paraphernalia stowed in the car and joined the eight other women in a cabin that nestled in a quiet wooded area lush with ferns and wildlife.

Because of my illness, I have had time to enjoy nature to an extent I never had before. Since both Emily and I enjoy nature, we frequently went for drives on the mountain, especially in the springtime when the rhododendron and mountain laurel blossoms were pushing through the leaves and covering the mountainside with color. When we parked and turned off the car, the evening sounds of waterfalls tumbling off the mountain and the birds calling to each other serenaded us and gave tranquility to our spirits. I closed my eyes and tried to store it all inside me—how I wished I could take it with me and pull it out while I lay in a hospital bed.

This weekend with friends held similar treasures that I hold in my heart. We walked, we talked, we played games, and we tasted of the goodness of nature and its Creator. We sat and watched the shy deer with their knobby-kneed fawns. We invested in each other's lives.

Singleness is a peculiar gift. The preacher of Ecclesiastes saw vanity, only vanity under the sun; yet, he proclaimed that "[God] hath made every thing beautiful in his time" (Ecclesiastes 3:11). Some singles struggle with feelings of emptiness and uselessness because they do not have a family of their own. "You are needed or you would not be here," others have told me, and I often tell it to myself. How can we impact the world and influence others in positive ways? I have found that opportunities lie everywhere if only we can find them. In fact, because of fewer responsibilities, we are free to connect with others and speak into their lives in ways that busy mothers are unable to. We can also make a difference for eternity by interacting with other people who have families. This can be done in many practical ways such as babysitting to give the parents a night out or baking for an overwhelmed and weary mother. They will be quick to recognize, perhaps before we do, the freedom and rich opportunity that comes with the gift of singleness.

Still, singleness can bring with it a sense of vulnerability because of the aloneness; that vulnerability stands as an invitation to fellowship with our Creator. In the perfect cosmos of Eden, the man and the woman walked and talked with God. Although the human race moved away from God and now suffers the consequences, we still are created to walk and talk with God. Being alone increases the hunger for that intimacy, and God has pronounced a blessing on those who hunger and thirst—for they shall be filled. Although I don't expect to stop hungering and thirsting until I get to heaven, I have often watched God supply the daily bread for my emotional needs.

Chapter 20

I lay in the hospital again with pancreatitis.

"Hey, sweetie, you've been in here too often. How are you feeling today?" asked one of my favorite nurses after she saw my name at the desk. The medical staff knew me by now, and I knew them.

"I don't feel too sweet today," I admitted. It was the day of my brother's wedding, and I was stuck in the hospital.

"Oh, I'm so sorry. May I pray with you?" the nurse asked.

"Yes, please do."

She prayed a very nice prayer for me and shed a few tears as she let herself feel my frustration. While she was on duty, she frequently stuck her head in the door, smiled, and went on with her work. Her love and understanding raised my spirits, and I recognized that once again God had filled me with the strength I needed to face the ordeal that came next.

Because of how difficult it was to find my veins, and after they found one, to keep the IV line in it, they decided to put a central line in my chest for more direct access to my heart. This would allow them to draw blood or give me IV fluids and medication without hours of pricking and poking me with their needles.

"Oh, no," I thought when I saw the student doctor step forward. I could have cried. He had a difficult time getting it placed correctly. He pushed and probed, gingerly pushing the line in and then pulling it back out until my nerves were nearly shot. Finally, the resident doctor took over and did the job.

"Sorry about that," he apologized as they left. Soon after that, I had trouble breathing. The doctor took me for an X-ray and, after looking at it, jerked to attention. "Who's Arlene's nurse?" he demanded. "Put her on oxygen and take her to the Step Down Unit immediately!" They had hit my left lung while installing the central line and now feared a lung collapse. This one time, the worst did not happen: the lung did not collapse, and I did not need to have another tube put in.

Since I now had a central line inserted in my chest and no longer needed to have others trying to find veins so they could give medication and IV fluids, the doctor suggested that I could learn to give myself TPN (Total Parenteral Nutrition). That meant I could go home and give myself my own IVs. Because any food or water I took in by mouth gave me pancreatitis, the doctor strictly forbade it, and I was willing to do anything to avoid pancreatitis. He also sent a morphine pump home with me. Both it and the TPN bags became my constant companions.

The social worker advocating for me proved to be an enormous help. She came with questions concerning what I would need in order to be comfortable after I left the hospital and arranged for Garrett County Home Health Care to come out to my house to explain all the procedures and equipment. She had also spoken with my insurance company, and they refused to pay for my supplies unless they were shipped from Baltimore, three hours away. It seemed ridiculous not to get them locally, but the TPN alone cost seven hundred dollars a day, so I was more than willing to put up with a little absurdity if they would pay for it. My apartment now looked like a hospital, but I liked being able to care for myself in this way, and it made me feel less useless and burdensome.

In the seven months from February to August 2005, I was admitted to the hospital five times and spent 65 days in the hospital because of pancreatitis. This, it seemed, provided more than enough reasons to move on and surgically remove my pancreas. My surgeon, Dr. Beachy, recognized we were quickly running out of other options. He asked to meet with the family the next day, and although they had jobs, my siblings declared that did not matter; they were ready to do anything they could to help me feel better. I do not know what I would do without their constant support and am eternally indebted to them.

My family suffered with me when pancreatitis flared up. They wished they could do something to ease my pain, but they could only sit with me, or, in some cases, drive fast! Miriam was driving to Grant Town and following my pleas to "please hurry," when lights began flashing in her rear view mirror. The officer jumped out of his car and waved his hat at us as though he expected us to take off before he got to us.

"Do you know how fast you were going?" he asked Miriam.

"No. My sister is in terrible pain, and I need to get her to the hospital. We have to go to Grant Town."

"You have no business going over the speed limit. I can get you an ambulance, but speeding is not an option. Even the ambulance isn't licensed to travel over the speed limit." He stooped down and looked in at me and asked, "What seems to be the problem?" but his voice did not sound very sympathetic. He certainly did not rush his paperwork, either, and he fined Miriam ninety dollars.

My sister-in-law Regina also got stopped once on a fast trip to Grant Town. When she saw the lights behind her, her frustration spilled out in tears. It was torture for her to see me in such pain, and when she did the only thing she knew to do, she received a fine she could hardly afford.

Now they all gathered at the hospital to hear what Dr. Beachy had to say. I had learned to trust Dr. Beachy in a way similar to how I had depended on Dr. Ohler for years. Certainly God had a hand in providing the doctors I needed. He spoke now while we sat quietly, hoping for a clear understanding for what we should do.

"We're looking at the possibility of an eight to twelve hour surgery called a Whipple operation to remove your pancreas and reroute your digestive system. It's a very serious step, but here's the story. If we don't do surgery, there is no hope. If we do surgery, there is not much hope. We can do this surgery and remove the pancreas, but we'll likely be exchanging one problem for a host of others. The pancreas makes insulin, and if we take it out, she will become a brittle diabetic and need regular insulin shots and will need to stay away from sugar. She will also run the risk of losing her eyesight or maybe an arm or leg because of uncontrolled diabetes. We don't know what will happen, but these concerns are why we have been so hesitant about removing the pancreas. The good news would be that you could no longer get pancreatitis. I know you've been through a lot with that."

Decisions are part of life: which house should I buy, how much money should I spend on a car, where should I attend college, should I take this job or hope for another? Now I faced a decision about what to do with my body. If I did not want to live with this pain forever, and I did not, it seemed I had no choice but to remove the pancreas. But the risks looked huge, and by now I knew that if I stayed true to form, I would face problems they had not even imagined. *Oh, Lord,* I pled, *show me what I need to do and then let me rest in that decision.* I held my Bible tightly against my chest as though that would press its words more deeply into my heart. I closed my eyes tightly, depending on God to intercede for me when I had no words to speak.

We made the decision to allow them to remove my pancreas because it only made my life miserable, and it seemed that if I knew I had done all I could, it might be easier to cope with whatever happened. Although I did not call up that telemarketer who had tried to sell me a burial plan, I did make sure that my living will was up to date. I did not know what would happen in the next month. Even after choosing surgery, I doubted and dreaded and feared what might happen, and because my body was worn down, the tempter wanted to take advantage of those broken defenses. Depression tried to sneak in every chance it got, and I felt too tired to fight it. It is in times like these and for reasons like these that I need other people's prayers.

Chapter 21

I tried hard to hide my concerns about my illness, thinking that my family experienced enough stress. Certainly, without their love and presence, I would have lost my way long ago. Two days before my surgery, James and Joanna became proud parents of another little girl, and they named her Jenell Arlene. My cousin in Tennessee had also named a new baby Arlene in honor of me. Even in ways like these, God shows His love for me by reminding me how many people care.

When I'm weary and feel I am running out of options for my life, my mind quickly gets stuck in downward spirals. "What purpose can this suffering possibly serve? It's just keeping me from doing what I enjoy. My life makes no difference in the world. I am only a burden."

Getting stuck on the question "why" sets me on a treadmill rather than a road leading toward God, but accepting the responsibility to do all I can for myself and finding small things to do for others, like making the frazzled nurse smile, keeps me feeling much more positive. I am truly handicapped only when I fail to use what I do have. Even when I do all the right things, however, courage and strength and grace to deal with suffering ultimately come from God, often because of the prayers of His people.

The nurse who greeted me as I went in for surgery laughed at the twelve-inch stack of paper that made up my medical records. "We might need to cut another tree!" she teased.

After the paperwork was complete and the medical staff, following protocol, once again covered the risks involved, I could not help wondering if I was making the right decision. Most people rest in the knowledge that rarely do all the possible side effects happen. I know that I will probably experience the side effects listed and more. We had committed it to God, so why was I having second thoughts? Jesus' words came to me: "Do not worry about tomorrow, for tomorrow will worry about itself. Each day has enough trouble of its own" (Matthew 6:34, NIV).

Just before they wheeled me into surgery, we all joined our hands as one of my ministers from church prayed. In spite of our tears and anxiety, we also felt a quietness inside that was possible only because of our confidence that an omniscient God was ultimately in control.

More than seven hours later, Dr. Beachy walked into the waiting room where my tired, anxious family sat, hoping for good news. He told them that the surgery had gone well. Most of that problematic pancreas was now gone, but the insulin-producing tip had still looked healthy, and he could not bring himself to remove it, hoping that diabetes would not be an immediate problem.

Drifting in and out of consciousness, I heard the drip, drip, drip from my intravenous infusion. Then Mom's voice reached me. "Arlene, how do you feel?" she asked. "The nurse said you're stable, and you seem to be resting. It's 2:30 in the morning, and we're going to be going home, but we'll be back first thing in the morning. I love you, dear."

I nodded. That's all I had the strength for.

A student nurse came in with a spirometer and insisted I do some breathing exercises. I closed my eyes and concentrated on breathing as gently as I could so I could bear the pain. I did want to cooperate but sometimes it was so hard. After a few more of her visits, I got annoyed. There was no reason for this student nurse to come in every thirty minutes to make me do breathing exercises when I could finally rest. I concluded she needed something to do. "Go pick on somebody else for a while," I seethed inside.

By the time my family came in the next morning, tears were trickling down my swollen and puffy face. Around the clock for the next six weeks, someone from my family stayed with me, suffering with me and doing anything they could to relieve my pain. They repositioned my pillows, turned me from side to side, swabbed my dry mouth and parched lips—anything to help me bear this terrific, nearly unbearable pain. Three days after surgery, I moved from my bed, hoping the motion would shift the gas trapped inside my body. It took several nurses to help me because of my five pumps, two poles, and three drainage bags. I always hit my morphine button before moving at all. That little tip of the pancreas had become inflamed, causing excruciating pain and trapping me in a nightmare of pain for weeks. Also, because the pancreas lies deep under the stomach and next to the spine, a surgery like this one involves a lot of manipulation, and my stomach became hard and enlarged because of the trapped gas inside. The pain from the twelve-inch incision seemed minor compared to what was going on inside.

The pain distressed me, but so did the fact that my family needed to give so much time to my care. Mom or Miriam were there, ready day or night to help me get up and walk around, trying to ease my pain. Mom recorded some of her feelings:

> Watching Arlene suffer so intensely day after day was tearing my heart into shreds. No matter what I did for her, she still suffered terribly. After nine days with almost no sleep for either of us, I was helplessly standing beside her bed at three o'clock in the morning and the dam broke. I wept, "Oh, Lord, where are You? Why, oh why have You deserted us so completely? People are praying. I am praying. But it seems You don't hear or care. We can't take this much longer."
>
> Deep inside I knew God did care, but I couldn't feel any of His love; I felt totally deserted and alone, and the anguish was crushing me. I needed to feel His presence. I needed His assurance. But where was it? Perhaps I was tasting a small part of the agony my Savior felt on the

cross when He asked, "My God, my God, why hast thou forsaken me?" (Matthew 27:46).

When I later described this experience to a friend, she replied, "I think we're allowed to ask God that question. Jesus Himself told God that He felt forsaken." A. B. Simpson wrote, "Here is the secret of divine all-sufficiency, to come to the end of everything in ourselves and in our circumstances. When we reach this place, we will stop asking for sympathy because of our hard situation or bad treatment, for we will recognize these things as the very condition of our blessing" (A. B. Simpson).

After four long weeks, I began feeling some better. Just maybe I would make it to David's wedding after all. But that was not going to happen. Once again, I had the doctors baffled, and they ordered more tests. I was taken to the radiology room and lay on the cold, hard X-ray table. "It shouldn't take longer than ten minutes," the nurse said.

Soon they were having fun. "Look at this!" they exclaimed to each other as they looked at the pictures. They got excited trying to find where the surgeon had made all the connections during my Whipple surgery. "Where in the world did they connect that? It's working backwards! Oh, here's . . . she's missing . . . I can't believe this . . .No wonder she's in pain!"

"Yeah," I thought. "I'm in pain, can't you see?" More students joined them and furthered their education. I had learned to like most nursing students because they were often eager to please and tried anything they could to make patients comfortable. Sometimes, however, they seemed to have no common sense or sensitivity and studied me like a textbook.

I was finding out that I had become quite a curious specimen, and after a very long hour, they finally let me go back to bed.

They did find the source of my pain, a serious bile leak close to where my pancreas had been removed. Some of the bitter gastric juices were escaping and collecting in the abdominal cavity, causing inflammation and pain which words cannot quite describe. They warned me that they might need to do another surgery to remedy the problem, but because of prayer and the goodness of God, it began to heal without surgery. I knew that apart from a miracle from God I would never again have a healthy body. After all, doctors had gone in and removed organs, essentially playing the part of Creator.

Once again, the love from a huge support network overwhelmed me. Friends took Mom to the cafeteria, helped with transportation, or gave money for gas and food. I received cards, flowers, and visitors. Visitors can be an encouragement, and a visit of a few minutes can do wonders. But a visit to a very ill patient can easily be overdone. Those visitors who travel far might think they ought to make their visits worthwhile by staying a bit longer, but I found they were appreciated more, not less, if they left before tiring me out. I found that before I had really recovered, I enjoyed visits most if others could carry on the conversation without expecting me to add much. Still, healthy people with normal lives cannot understand how much the little things mean. People who listen, write, send a card, or give a hug are giving the greatest gifts that will never be forgotten.

One day, when I was in severe pain without even a brief respite, I finally called out to the desk again. I thought I could not take it any longer. The nurse came in and burst out, "You already have all the medication you may have." She then turned on her heels and was gone. Before that, I'd thought her to be a kind and sensitive nurse. I poured out my distress to Mom: "They just don't seem to care at all. If they could experience it for just fifteen minutes, they would understand."

Later the same nurse met Mom in the hall and said, "After I left her room, I just wept. I can't stand seeing her suffering for weeks and feeling I can't do anything about it. It's just not right. It's not fair! Why does she have to suffer so much?"

The next setback was an infection at the site of the incision. My spirits dropped, and I felt tears trickling down my face. Just then, one of my favorite nurses stepped in. She listened while I vented. "Isn't life ever going to get any better? Did we make the right decision?" I do not remember the words she spoke to me that day, but she gave me the courage to go on. She could not possibly have realized what joy she had brought into the dull hospital room that morning. God knew I needed her.

Chapter 22

"Mom, something isn't right. It sounds crazy, but I feel like my insides are shaking but my skin is standing still. I feel like my bowels need to move, but they don't." For the next hour, Mom unplugged and plugged my pumps as she helped me to and from the bathroom. Then I started vomiting and feeling totally miserable.

Western Maryland University's college football game had drawn thousands of sports fans into Grant Town, and Mom stood at my window with her back to me, watching the game which was going on across the hospital parking lot as though she had totally forgotten that I was there. After a little, I told her I was feeling alone and as though the game were more important than I was.

She turned to me, distress written on her face. "Arlene, I am sorry, I just feel so helpless. I don't know what to do for you, so I was just standing here praying for you. I'm going to go get a nurse.

The nurse and a doctor followed Mom back into my room and almost immediately saw that my morphine pump had quit working, and I was going through a withdrawal. It took several doses to get me back up on top, and it seemed rather strange to know how addicted I had become to my pain medication. Even with all the morphine I took, I lived with nearly constant pain.

As the nursing staff learned to know me over the years, they did their best to get me a private room, but sometimes none was available. Anytime I had a roommate, I wondered how I could let them know more about God. This time, I felt like a wimp with all my moaning and groaning. "What kind of a testimony is this?" I thought.

I had a brief conversation with my roommate who had had her

first baby three weeks before, then acquired an infection and needed to be on IV antibiotics. She felt she was breaking down. Her father was helping her husband take care of the infant, and the young mother worried constantly, calling home every few hours. "How is she doing? What is she doing? Make sure her bottle is warm. Did you remember to change her Pamper?"

The following evening I overheard her telling her husband what she had learned about me from brief conversations between me and Mom or from overhearing the doctors talking.

"This girl is twenty-eight and has been sick most of her life, in and out of the hospital constantly. She hurts and it always takes them so long to bring her pain medication. I called out a couple times for her and still had no response. She never swears and never complains. She has a caring family, friends, and a pastor that comes to visit and pray with her. It's wonderful! I think we better start going to church again. Since we quit attending church, everything is going wrong."

In spite of my weakness, this exciting response cheered me. Despite her exclamation that "it's wonderful!" I felt right then that my life was anything but wonderful. My brother was getting married, and I wouldn't be there to witness it. I endured the day, and when David and Becky stopped in to see me as they left for their honeymoon, I felt that I had in a small way been able to share in their happy day.

Ruth, another roommate, never had visitors. After a couple weeks, Mom asked her if she had any family or friends or if we could do something for her.

"They dropped me off at the ER, and I don't know where they went. Can you call this number for me? I don't know why my boyfriend never calls or comes to see me." Nobody answered the phone when Mom called.

Ruth got no cards except for the card Mom gave her. She had no visitors except for my visitors. No pastor prayed for her except when my pastor prayed for her. When she was discharged from the hospital, they took her by ambulance to a nursing home because they had no information on her or anyone who might care for her. Sharing one of my flower arrangements with her felt like such a small token of love for a life starved for belonging, but she was delighted.

Ruth had often called out to the desk, "Come change my bed." Some of the nurses became annoyed with her, and Joe, the orderly, lost his patience and snapped, "Why don't you either go to the bathroom or use the bedpan? This could be prevented!"

"I can't walk."

"You could if you just would," he fumed. "I'm going to let you lie in it for awhile. That'll teach you!" Another time, he actually smacked her. I wondered if I should report him, but I didn't want him taking care of me after I squealed on him. Joe frequently came into my room and sat down to talk. I didn't feel well enough to want to listen to his long list of complaints, and I always wondered who was waiting for help while he sat in my room running his mouth and making more work for the rest of the staff. When I told him I was going home, he offered to take me. I told him I had a ride, thank you very much!

Joe was eventually fired, and I must say I thought that was a wise decision.

After six weeks in the hospital, I went home with no tubes attached, but I figured some strings were attached to this good deal. I just didn't know what they were or what would pull me back to the hospital again.

I thoroughly enjoyed my ride home. When I left for surgery, the leaves were green; now the trees were raining leaves in many brilliant colors. When I pulled into the driveway at home, I was convinced the leaves there were the most beautiful leaves I'd ever seen anywhere in my life. It had been so many years since I played in the crisp, fallen leaves with my sisters and complained about the apples dropping on our heads. The fresh air and the smells and sounds of the country provided such a delightful change from my hospital world that I wondered what it would be like when I traveled from this life to the next. I guessed the feelings would be something like this. Oh, how I would welcome that change! The tunnel of pain and illness between me and my childhood looked so long and narrow. I wondered what the future held.

Chapter 23

Five months after my pancreas came out, I again started experiencing nausea and weight loss. Dr. Howard told me to go, as he says, "to see the boys in Grant Town." I called the doctor to set up an appointment. "Hello, I am calling to make an appointment," I started, then suddenly got the feeling I had maybe dialed the wrong number.

"I don't think you want an appointment with us. This is the funeral home. Why don't you try again?"

I got a good laugh out of that misplaced call!

After another try, I was told to come in to the hospital the following afternoon. I was admitted because my food intake, though it was all my stomach would handle, was not enough to keep me going.

"Oh, no!" the nurse said as she set her glasses down on her nose. "I remember you from before. You have no veins. We need blood work done and an IV started for hydration. They're also waiting for an IV access to inject the dye for the CT scan." She looked but did not even see anything to prick. "You won't like me for this, but we have to put a central line in your upper chest again." She was right; I did not like it. In fact, I hated it.

Because of the danger of hitting the lung while placing the line, I had papers to sign. After tedious work and lots of discomfort in spite of their efforts to numb me, the central line was working. After the CT scan was completed, I wondered why they were rushing me upstairs. Several doctors and nurses met me at the elevator door, and I understood that they had punctured my lung again.

"Shall I call your family?" a nurse asked.

"I think I'll be okay. I don't want to bother them if I don't need to. If it gets serious, we can call them."

"Honey, they want a chest tube placed," the nurse told me with sympathy in her voice.

I tried to argue the doctor out of it, but he still insisted it be done immediately.

"But why can't you sedate me?" I asked.

"We don't have time to waste getting you sedated," he said. Air was already accumulating between the lining of the lungs and the chest wall cavity, causing the lung to collapse. The chest tube would suck the air from the cavity and give the lung room to expand. With yet more stress and hard work, the chest tube was placed. They monitored me closely until I was out of the danger zone. All this had taken place during the night, and I was ready for a rest and some sleep. I finally got to my room, and there on the bedside stand lay a single velvety red rose. It was positively beautiful.

Early in the morning, the student doctor who had placed the tube peeked around the pulled curtain. With a startled expression, he looked at my chest tube, then turned and left without a word. He must not have known until he saw me that he had hit the lung.

They now needed to let the lung heal before they could do anything else. The next step would probably need to be exploratory surgery. They just could not figure out what was actually happening inside.

"How about putting in a zipper?" I asked Dr. Beachy.

Exploratory surgery was the last thing I wanted to think about, yet it was hardly a surprise. I went in for surgery at the appointed time, only to find out that my surgery had been rescheduled without our knowing it, although they claimed they had tried calling the day before. Miriam and Wes went to town and bought a card game to help pass the time.

"Okay, dear, we are ready for you. Dr. Beachy will also be placing a Broviac, a more permanent line that gets routed into the heart for blood work, fluids, and some medications. These central lines don't last long," the nurse explained. "The doctor is also saying that since it looks like you will be dependent on TPN for the rest of your life, the Broviac makes a lot of sense."

Because of the chances for infection, Broviacs are placed only when absolutely necessary, but I could not help thinking of how many hours of trouble it would have saved me if I had had it earlier. Having nurses and doctors sticking needles into one's body for hours on end, trying to find a vein, is no fun.

As I came back to consciousness after surgery, one of the first things I asked was what they found. By now I knew my illness was not psychological, but the repercussions of what some people had inferred about me or had wondered within themselves still stayed with me. I wanted to know I had not just imagined my pain.

Dr. Beachy had not run into as much scar tissue as he had expected, but they had done a lot of stitching, patching, redirecting, and re-stitching my poor digestive tract. They had also removed part of the stomach and small intestines and loaded me up with tubes. The J-tube led into the jejunum, or small intestines, through which they hoped eventually to feed me, instead of running TPN through my IV. The G-tube went directly into the stomach for draining the gastric juices that accumulate in the stomach. And he had inserted the Broviac. These three tubes would stay with me indefinitely.

"Mom? Hey, Mom?" I looked over at her and saw she was in a deep sleep. The dear woman's around-the-clock nursing had exhausted her, so I called for the nurse aide to come walk with me to hopefully rid myself of some gas pain. She took me for the walk and then helped me back into bed while Mom still slept, oblivious to what went on around her.

Living in hospitals has a way of opening one's eyes to those who have the ministry of encouragement. One man walked through the halls and played a harp he had strung himself, serenading patients with lovely, relaxing hymns. Knowing how much I enjoyed it, he started to watch the computer for my name in the list of patients so he would be sure to come play for me. The soft music always relaxed me on rough days.

Once in a while I met another patient whose story shone with God's grace and proclaimed the message of triumph in suffering that

I hoped my own life would give. Lisa was one woman like that. She was an only child whose parents were deceased. She had never married and was nearly alone in the world. She now battled the Flesh-Eating Disease, a bacterial infection that releases toxins that destroy skin and muscles. When we met her, she was facing another surgery to clean out the infected flesh and do more skin grafting. The prognosis looked pretty bleak, but Lisa had a beaming testimony for her great God, whom she still trusted, loved, and served. Church activities like Bible studies helped her fight off depression.

After Lisa was discharged and came back for an appointment, she brought in a basket for me filled with toiletries like soap, lotion, and a booklet of Bible helps. She modeled exactly what I wanted to be. Instead of fussing and fuming, she did what she could.

Hospital life sometimes seems a bit like family life as everyone needs to deal with everyone else's moods. Mom was stuck in the hospital again as a blizzard dumped down snow and blew it over the roads. I would be receiving no visitors today, although David and Becky had gone ten miles before landing in a ditch and deciding to turn back. Being snowbound in hospitals is not much fun, and some of the nurses who couldn't get home stayed double shift, making a tired, grouchy staff.

Eventually, the tubes caused problems. Every time my dressings needed to be changed, the agonizing pain made me sweaty and weak. "Hi, Arlene. I just discharged you six weeks ago. What are you doing to yourself?" my social worker teased.

My Broviac line looked great, but the skin around both the J and G tubes was raw from the draining gastric juices. The size of the tubes worsened the situation by constantly rubbing against the raw areas, causing much pain. Home Health Care came out daily to change the dressings, and I dreaded it terribly. They prescribed extra morphine to be taken thirty minutes before the nurses arrived for the dressing change, but I still nearly screamed while they worked. The road to recovery was rough. For three months the nurses came to my house seven days a week to change my dressings.

Because any movement brought irritation and any irritation brought horrible pain, I spent hours and hours on the sofa. From where I lay inside the door, I could watch the birds in the trees outside the door. Once again, nature worked its miracle and brought a deep peace and a confirmation of God's love. I learned to identify with other people who have dealt with long-term illness and who say that at first, cards, flowers, phone calls, and visitors are frequent. All too soon, however, the mailbox is empty, the phone silent, and the guest book dusty. Then reality steps in and one needs to accept that this is just the way it is going to be.

There are some beautiful exceptions, though, and I felt so blessed and encouraged when Lena started stopping in regularly. I hadn't been able to attend Sunday school for many months, so on Monday afternoons I could expect a visit from seventy-year-old Lena. She filled me in on what they had discussed. She also stayed with me sometimes to give my family time free from my care. She became a dear friend to me.

During this time, my teeth and eyes started causing problems. When I was a child, Dad spent a lot of money on my teeth, but since I became ill, they were rapidly decaying, and it was becoming a losing battle. My dentist referred me to the School of Dentistry at Grant Town. Dr. Morgan always had a warm smile and a cheery whistle while he worked. Because I had taken in little food orally for the past eight years and did not have the natural saliva flow for healthy teeth and gums, I had a too-dry mouth. "I'm going to write you a prescription for saliva," he said.

I gave him a queer look when he handed it to me.

"Chuckling, he assured me, "It's artificial saliva."

A year later, Dr. Morgan decided that trying to fix my teeth was futile. The older dentist who removed my teeth made me laugh, chattering nonstop. After he had my mouth full of his instruments, he still talked and asked questions while I grunted in reply. This process was no fun, but I've had much worse things done to me.

I began noticing that my eyesight seemed to be deteriorating rapidly, and the doctor sent me to the Eye Institute connected to the hospital in Grant Town. Again I found myself fortunate to live close to one of three specialized optometry units in the United States. The office was beautiful, with tall trees growing toward the high ceilings. Each testing unit had its own waiting room with free coffee and cookies.

They scheduled me for a test that required me to stay awake for twenty-four hours prior to the test. I wondered how I could accomplish that feat, particularly since I am not exactly an active person.

My tubes and pumps slow me down even when I do feel comfortable moving. Then a mother called me up with a brilliant plan. Her young daughters invited some of their friends for a sleep over—at my house! Since the girls had school the next morning, they slept in shifts and had jolly times in between. By the time I got to the Eye Institute for my appointment, they had what they wanted: a very sleepy woman. They wanted to measure the electrical impulses of the brain in a relaxed state.

The conclusion the doctor reached from the many test results made me sigh. "As you were recovering from your major surgery, there was too much pressure behind your eyes from trying to endure the severe pain. Since that is what is causing your vision loss, there's nothing I can do about it."

I was beginning to feel as normal as I ever expected to get with all my tubes, so I held high hopes that I would be able to see my sister get married. Miriam had announced her engagement to Wes. They planned their wedding for the fall. I was excited when they bought a house close to my apartment. Knowing they would be close by gave me a welcome sense of security.

She declared that we would never be able to surprise her with a bridal shower; she was too smart to let us sneak it past her. Martha had a brilliant plan. We would have the bridal shower the same week our family had planned a weekend vacation at a cabin in West Virginia. Anyone knew it would be insane to try having a shower in the middle of packing up for vacation! Invitations were sent out for a one p.m. party. On the day of the shower, Joanna called and wondered if someone could help her get ready to go to Canaan Valley that afternoon. Mom relayed the message and assured Miriam that she and Martha could manage the work at home.

The minute she walked out the door, we moved into high gear, preparing the decorations and refreshments. At just the right time, Joanna thanked Miriam for her help and asked her to stop by James' shop with a package on her way home. The minute Miriam left, Joanna gathered up the children, strapped them into their car seats, and drove to Mom's house. She sneaked into the basement and upstairs just in time to see Miriam running down the steps to the house. The moment she opened the door we shouted, "Surprise!" Her blue eyes popped as we burst into gales of laughter at the flabbergasted look on her face. She hid her face behind the door, trying to readjust her mind. "We don't have time for this," she murmured. We felt highly accomplished that day.

After the party, we finished packing up and headed for Canaan Valley. As soon as the vehicles stopped, the excited youngsters were out and racing to explore every nook and cranny, reserving sleeping spots before we had even had time to unload. When it was actually time to sleep, though, they were far too excited to settle down easily. The weekend held fun: playing volleyball, kickball, boating, and otherwise reveling in the joys of vacation time. It included some unwelcome excitement. Suddenly, from my perch on the sandy shore underneath an umbrella, I heard a scream and commotion down by the lake. Martha and Andrew had gone on a boat ride and were back on shore. I looked in time to see Andrew getting up out of the water dripping wet! Martha had accidentally dumped him into the lake when she stepped out of the boat.

It seemed every single time we got together for special family time something happened so that I needed to go to Grant Town to the hospital that had become my second home. This time was no exception. I was terribly disappointed, but my J-tube seemed to be clogged. I just could not understand why it had to happen now.

While they were trying to decide who would go with me, the frustration with being a constant bother brought tears to my eyes. The problem was fixed and we were able to rejoin the family for the remainder of the weekend. Shortly before we left, someone spied a bear cub digging through the garbage can on the deck, unaware of his enthralled audience. We watched, fascinated. Finally satisfied with what he found, he lumbered across the parking lot and into the edge of the woods with his treasure—a dirty Pamper! The belly laughs we got out of that one ended the vacation on the right note.

Chapter 24

I woke from a catnap one evening in the springtime of 2000 feeling decidedly strange. My arms and legs felt like Jell-O, and I had little control of my arms. I didn't know how I could get to the phone, but I flailed my arms and legs and somehow hit the right button on the phone to get Emily's attention. I found I could not speak, but Emily immediately detected trouble and came running downstairs.

"What shall I do?"

When I was unable to respond, she quickly called the ambulance and soon I was on the way to Grant Town. They believe I experienced a mini-stroke, but amazingly enough, I was out of the hospital in five days with no serious side effects from the stroke. How I thanked God for that gift!

Since I had become a diabetic, my sugar levels fluctuated so drastically and changed so quickly that it was becoming dangerous for me to stay alone. Mom stopped by to check my sugar levels on the way to a school play. When she came back, she came to the door and found it locked.

"Arlene!" she yelled. My lights were on, but I wasn't answering. She looked for a peephole in the blind, and when she saw me sitting on my recliner with my head dangling limply, she was sure I was in insulin shock. Mom checked all the doors, but the house was locked up and Emily was at work. She walked up to the neighbors and called Miriam.

By the time she got back to the house, Wes and Miriam were checking my sugar level. It was dangerously low, so they ran to get a glucose shot. Each injection cost $200.00. They decided to wait to see if I was coming out of shock. Fifteen minutes later I still was not responding, so they called the ambulance.

I was now officially a diabetic and started taking insulin shots regularly. It was amazing, really, that I had gone without the shots as long as I did after the Whipple operation. Because of my wildly irregular sugar levels, Wes and Miriam fixed up their basement as an apartment so they could keep a close watch on me. Mom helped when she could. Although I could see that moving into their basement was a wise idea, I found it hard to acknowledge that I really needed that kind of help. I felt I was giving up another chunk of my independence. Perhaps I gave it up a bit grudgingly, but I definitely appreciated all that Wes and Miriam did for me.

Always ready to try anything that might help my situation, I decided, with Dr. Rifes' permission, to see if someone at the Cleveland Clinic in Ohio would be able to help me. I was scheduled to see three doctors, and on Monday morning the doctor at the pain clinic said he could do no more for me than what was being done. From there, I went for a lengthy appointment with the GI doctor, who had been researching the possibilities of snipping the nerve that sends pain impulses to the brain from the pancreas. He was looking for someone like me who would be willing to let him try it.

"But what would happen if I became seriously ill and didn't know it because I had no pain?" I asked. He acknowledged the seriousness of the implications but seemed somewhat annoyed that I wasn't immediately jumping for his offer. I just felt tired of being an experiment for research. The next morning, I went for my last appointment in Cleveland, this one concerning my diabetes. My sugar readings alternately ran too high and too low, rarely staying in the happy medium range. That doctor made some minor recommendations for changing my insulin, but he supported the methods we were using. We came home with few additional answers, but we did have more confidence that we were indeed doing all within our power. Resting in the knowledge of God's control seems right when I have done all I reasonably can.

My family had come to Wes' for a fun time of being together. Since

I was not feeling well, I went downstairs to rest for a while, hoping and praying the discomfort would pass. The painful muscle spasms under and around my ribs did not fit my usual list of symptoms. My stomach was large and swollen tight, though, and as it pushed up under my ribs, I had difficulty breathing easily. When I thought I had reached the limit of my endurance, I called upstairs.

Mom and Miriam came down, and we decided to call the ambulance. Soon I started gasping for breath. Legally, they were required to take me to the closest hospital, so I headed for Bear Creek Hospital. What must have been a forty-five minute ride at most seemed like hours. They could not find the right adapters to access my Broviac, so I had no morphine to help with the agonizing pain.

Beth, one of the ambulance crew members, made me grin despite it all when she said, "Arlene, if I didn't know better, I would declare you are in labor!" She sat with me, stroking my arm and even shedding tears with me. "I can't stand watching you hurt like this, dear. Just hang in there; you'll make it!" I sat up, lay down, stood up, and turned from one side to the other as I desperately searched for a comfortable position. I thought I would never get through this pain alive. And who knows, maybe I would not have if Beth had not been there. She was such a lifesaver! Her care calmed my mind even though she could do nothing for my body, and she never made me feel like a fussy child.

Dr. Thom met me in the hallway as they wheeled me in. Soon the morphine was on its way. They decided that I was suffering from another bowel blockage although they had no explanation for the severe muscle spasms. With my belly so big and tight, my heart experienced extreme pressure and struggled to get the oxygen to my body.

On a normal person, the smooth muscles are like little fingers squeezing matter down through the esophagus, stomach, and small intestine and on to the large intestine. In my case, the smooth muscles were lax and ineffective. The narcotics I had been on for ten years to ease the discomfort of the sluggish system had slowed it down further. On top of that, one of the X-rays showed a hernia at the site of a previous surgery. As though that were not quite enough, my J-tube was broken. I was so weary of tests and exasperated with my pain, my pancreas, the helpless doctors, and other things. As I once more turned it over to God, recognizing that He was in ultimate control, the fear left me and peace filled me.

Over the years, I have found roommates can be a blessing. I've received cards and gifts from former roommates and their families. I remember one dear lady in particular who modeled the kind, consistently appreciative attitudes I want to show. Never once did a complaining word cross her lips, and no matter what was going on, she was a pleasure to have around. Nancy was a sweet little grandmother I kept in contact with. Her daughter-in-law asked if they could put my name on their church prayer list. Of course I didn't mind. Prayer had seen me through. I certainly did not object to more!

Before the doctor left for a day at the clinic, he stopped by to get my consent to go to Grant Town. My stomach continued growing larger and harder, and the medical staff at Grant Town agreed with Bear Creek. I gave my consent.

On a Sunday morning, an unfamiliar doctor was on call. He was talking before he even came around the curtain and could see me. "Arlene, you've been having problems with your bowels for a long time. It's time to do surgery to take part of your colon out."

What? I didn't know that's what they were thinking! The next morning I asked my regular doctor if I needed surgery. He shook his head and said that it was a possibility sometime in the future, but they were not ready to suggest that yet. What a relief that was! I had had several organs removed by now, and the agony I experienced after each surgery gave me a terror of similar surgeries.

My system had straightened itself out well enough that I was ready to get back home, but the J-tube still had not been replaced. The surgical team thought it was a job for Family Medicine, and Family Medicine expected the surgical team to do it. At long last, the right crew got with the job. They then needed to take me in my bed down to have the tube X-rayed to be sure it was in place.

"These beds are impossible to steer," one of them complained.

"Where's your driver's license for this thing?" I asked as we bumped into another wall.

"Hey, Arlene, you lost some of your belly," one of my nurses noticed as she stood to the side to let us pass her in the hallway. "You looked like you were close to delivering when you came into the hospital!" she said, making us all chuckle. It was wonderful to be feeling better again!

When one part of the body's system breaks down, we need to create human solutions to replace the natural plan. Those human solutions often bring more problems. But what alternative did we have? When one knows what real pain is, living in that torment is no option.

Chapter 25

When my IV line developed a leak, we had no choice but to go to Grant Town to the emergency room. Of course, it happened in the evening—problems always seemed to crop up on either evenings or weekends.

"So what is it this time?" the nurse asked as she got my vitals.

"I have a leak in my line."

"Let me see your book. It's quite a book you carry with you, with all your medications and medical history listed."

The ER doctor looked at the tube and said, "I'll get some cultures done to make sure there's not a line infection somewhere. As for the line, sometimes we can patch them, but with the location of this leak, I don't think we can. I'll call Dr. Pierce to request surgery immediately." Dr. Pierce had taken over Dr. Beachy's position.

While I waited for Dr. Pierce, John, a nursing student I remembered from the time I had my Whipple operation, walked by my room. Suddenly he stopped and backed up, then came in and gave me a big hug. "I remember you from ten years ago when you had all these tubes placed. We all honestly didn't think you would pull through. God truly must have a special mission for you whether you know it or not," he told me. I had surprised many people, many times.

"Did I get you out of bed tonight?" I asked when Dr. Pierce walked in.

"No, just off the couch where I was watching the football game."

I could live in continual guilt for the inconvenience I often am to others. One of the greatest challenges for the chronically ill patient is graciously accepting help and, at the same time, doing everything possible to help himself.

Surgery progressed quickly to replace the tube, and I got home again before dawn. Two days later, Grant Town called. The results from the culture they had taken showed I had a nasty bacterial infection growing in my blood. My blood platelets and white and red cell counts all came back low as well. As soon as I got to the hospital, they put me on five different IV antibiotics, hoping that whatever the problem was, they would have treated for it.

"Mom, I need to use the restroom. Will you bring my IV pole?" Getting up on the side of the bed, an unnatural feeling swept over me. "Mom, get the nurse. Quick." I had that crazy feeling again when I feel like I'm shaking on the inside while my skin stays still.

I had reacted to my medication, and my sugar count had gone up to 720, normal being between 80 and 120.

"Why, with readings like that, am I still talking sensibly?" I asked the nurse.

"Good question. I don't know, but you're definitely a tough one."

Four weeks later, I was discharged with orders to continue two different IV antibiotics for ten more weeks. I was fortunate to have come out of that ordeal unscathed.

When the sweet corn matures in the fall, the Kauffman family holds one gigantic corn day. We gather at Wes' garage to husk, cook, wash, cut off, and freeze enough corn to last us for a year. By evening, everybody was tired, but they still had not seen the last of the corn. I wished I could help them, but my contribution for the day was to be as little trouble as possible. When the time came to prepare my TPN bags and get the IV line hooked up again, I thought that the least I could do was take care of myself and let my weary siblings stay at the job.

I injected the insulin into my arm and then froze with shocked dismay. That insulin needed to go into the TPN bag where it would run through the IV line over the next 24 hours, but I had just sent it all directly into my bloodstream! Horrified, all I could do was call for help. They did all they could to keep my glucose levels within the normal range of between 70 and 150 mg/dL, but all our efforts, including $600 worth of glucose shots, could not keep the numbers from dropping dangerously low. As we headed for the emergency room, the reading showed 35.

The next twelve hours were nightmarish until the glucose levels in my bloodstream finally leveled out and I could head home, feeling sorry that I had put my family through this ordeal. This disastrous attempt to be helpful reminded me of a childhood incident that Mom was able to laugh at only later.

"Okay, youngsters, I want you all to go to the garden and pull weeds from the row of lima beans until I have dinner ready," Mom instructed us.

Grabbing hoes, we took off and got busy. Thirty minutes later, I straightened up from pulling weeds and exclaimed, "We finished it all before lunch!"

Later in the afternoon Mom went out to the garden and suddenly drew in a breath of dismay. "Oh, no! Not my precious lima beans!" The nice row of lima beans was now a nice row of weeds. "Well, we'll just do without lima beans this year," decided Mom.

True to form, it was on a Sunday morning that I discovered a leak in my Broviac tube. Danny and Regina took me to Grant Town this time, leaving their children with their cousins except for six-month-old Benson, who came along and kept everyone entertained.

When the medical staff checked out the problematic tube, they noticed my belly was once again swollen big and tight. I'd decided not to mention it, hating to stretch out Danny and Regina's time in the hospital. Fourteen hours later, the doctor came with the report that I had another bowel blockage. They wanted to keep me for observation. At two a.m., my brother and his wife finally went home to their family, having once again shown me what an amazing family I have.

When I arrived on the seventh floor, a couple of nurses came in to say hi. "Hey, I remember you from ten years ago, on east hall," one of them said. "How are the nieces and nephews?"

Wow! I wondered what impression I had left that helped them remember me from so long ago.

Two weeks later, I went home again. The doctors had found only the same old questions with the same old inadequate answers.

The roads were closed off in Grant Town for a huge football game in November 2004 when I headed to the ER with chest pains and shortness of breath, my left leg dragging and stinging as though it were sleeping.

"Hi, Arlene!" I heard someone say.

"Diana! It sure is good to see your face!"

"I saw your name on the board by the desk and decided to take my break and come talk to you for a couple minutes. Tell you what, it's wild in here tonight, like usual on game nights. Diana always added vehement gestures and facial expressions to her exclamations. "Drunks, freak accidents, people slicing their wrists. One man smacked another on his face and needs stitches because the other guy bit him back. Another jumped off a high bridge and messed up his knee, and another fell into the fish tank in the middle of town. They do all kinds of insane things. They'd save themselves a lot of trouble if they'd only think twice, but they don't, so they pay for it. Don't try it, my girl," she chuckled and gave me a hug. "So how are you, really!"

I shrugged. "My sugar is out of control, and now my leg went numb on me."

She nodded. "It's probably poor circulation because of diabetes. Some people lose a limb, but we'll hope for the best." She looked into my face. "Well, I've got to get going. You look tired and stressed out. I never saw you like this before. You always look like everything's okay, but this time I detect a bit of discouragement. Keep your chin up, sweetie."

Did she think I was superhuman? She'd told me before that when I looked so composed, some people didn't understand the extent of my pain. I was admitted for pain control. My white blood count was too low, and my diabetes was flaring up, as was my chronic pancreatitis, and I felt anything but superhuman.

After a year with no GI doctor available in Grant Town, I was glad to get in touch with Dr. Rizer from Johns Hopkins Hospital in Baltimore. When I saw him in his office, he asked if I understood how serious my situation really was. All my scar tissue would never stop causing problems. I thought I probably knew as well as anyone how serious my illness was. I asked him if removing the rest of the pancreas would clear up the chronic pancreatitis pain, and although he promised to talk to the surgeon, he did not sound too hopeful.

"I'm afraid no one's going to want to do it with your medical history. I want to see you after Christmas, and by then I should have had a chance to talk to the surgeon. I hope you can have a merry Christmas despite all this. Don't eat too much," he chuckled. I had eaten little by mouth for eleven years.

On Christmas Day, I counted twenty-seven cards in my mailbox at church, which brought the total to at least ninety small signs that there were people who cared for me. As I thought of the year ahead, I allowed myself to look at the various possibilities for the future. I realized that what I feared the most was not the possibility of dying. The valley I feared was the continuation of pain with no prospect of relief. Medically, there was very little that could be done.

A visitor once asked me when I was in excruciating pain, "How can you do it?"

It is because God is a good and faithful God that I have been able to keep on living and loving. I love the Lord and trust Him, and I know for certain He knows what He is doing even though I certainly do not.

Chapter 26

"Hi, Arlene, how are you doing?" Dr. Rizer asked.

"Okay."

"Are you all right?" he asked again, wanting a deeper answer.

"Well, not quite, but I'm coping," I replied.

He had talked to the surgeons as he had promised, and nobody wanted to touch my belly with a ten-foot pole. Everything in the digestive system was messed up and nothing worked normally. "Do you have any questions?" he asked.

"Yes," I thought to myself, "but all my questions are for God."

Once, after a new doctor had been in to see me, a visitor told me the doctor had been pacing back and forth in the hallway outside my room before entering. "Poor doctors!" I thought. I had become quite a challenge and an education for them; they were often as frustrated as I was.

After an extremely rough day a month later, with pain coming and going until it finally became unbearable late in the evening, I was admitted to Bear Creek Hospital.

Again the usual tests were done, and the doctor came in with the results. An enlarged liver and spleen were causing the excruciating pain like a tight band around and under my ribs like open sores rubbing against each other. "We'll have to send you to Grant Town after we get you comfortable, hopefully in a few days," he said. "I'm guessing the problem is caused by your TPN. TPN is hard on the liver."

But TPN was the only way I got any nutrition! I felt like I had been trapped in a maze, with each passage bringing new and irrevocable consequences.

In the meantime, Mom was talking on the phone. "Oh, I had an appointment with the surgeon this forenoon to see about having my hernia surgery this week, but I'll see how Arlene is doing by then. I'll be over."

"Mom, what's going on?" I asked when she got off the phone.

Miriam had called, wondering if we had heard that Andrew and Martha were on their way to Memorial Hospital, several miles from where I was admitted. Martha, expecting a baby soon, had gone for a checkup. When they discovered that the baby's heartbeat was weak, they took her to the hospital, not knowing if the baby would make it."

"Arlene, will you be okay if I run over to Memorial Hospital for a while?" Mom asked. I could see she was torn, with two daughters in two hospitals.

"Yes, Mom, go. Martha needs you worse than I do right now." Dear, faithful Mom. She put off her hernia surgery until she thought her girls could do without her. It's quite the extraordinary family she has!

Martha was on my mind constantly until I found out ten hours later that baby Anthony was born by Caesarean section. Mother and baby were doing fine.

Since Martha had surgery, she would need help caring for the new baby and his four lively siblings. I would need somebody close by to continue watching for unexpected extremes in my glucose levels, and Mom would need some time and help as she recovered from her hernia surgery. Miriam had a plan for shuffling us that would help us all, so while I was in the hospital, Martha moved into my apartment where Miriam was close by. They stayed in my apartment until I was discharged. After I came home, Mom had her surgery and moved in with me. I took care of her and she took care of me, but really Miriam took care of both of us!

My brother Alton and his family were planning to head to Michigan that summer to work with troubled boys. We thought it was the perfect time for another family camp-out, but since money was a bit tight that year, someone had the idea to camp out in Wes's large backyard. Our makeshift camp turned out to be lots of fun for adults and youngsters.

Saturday afternoon I came into the trailer where the little girls were playing. "Are you sick?" I asked one of them who was lying on the floor.

"No, we're just playing sick. I am Arlene."

"Hey, we better call the ambulance," another little girl put in her appropriate contribution.

Miriam and Wes had given so much of their time to me. I knew I could never repay them, but now that they had two children, they realized they were going to be doing both me and them a disservice by not being able to give everyone the attention they needed. Also, Mom's back was causing her serious problems by this time. She was becoming no younger and would perhaps need care at some time.

God put the puzzle together for us in a way none of us could have foreseen. As one of the Proverbs states, "A man's heart deviseth his way: but the LORD directeth his steps" (Proverbs 16:9). This happened for us. Andrew and Martha were looking for a place to buy, and they hit upon a plan that took care of us all. Andrew's family would move into Mom's house so that Miriam would still be available to help but would be relieved of the constant care she now provided for me. It all sounded so perfect, but Mom knew me. "It's true Miriam needs more help and Arlene needs more care," she said one time while I was gone. "But I'm afraid Arlene isn't ready to move in with anybody. She likes her apartment and her privacy."

When they told me what they were thinking, I once again cringed at the knowledge that I needed so much care and was taking other people's time. I had lived alone for twenty years and knew that changing now would require me to make some real adjustments. Still, I felt that if my family thought this arrangement would work best, I should cooperate. I really depended on them, and I so badly wanted to avoid being a burden to others, though I knew I had failed so often to be the pleasant, grateful patient I wanted to be. I knew it would mean that Mom, too, would need to adjust to sharing a house with someone else again.

Andrew searched for and found a double-wide that could be sectioned into two parts. After I had made up my mind, I immediately started going through my things and packing up. "Arlene, you better slow down. You just go and go, and I'm afraid you're going to pay for it," Mom scolded.

On October 1, 2005, the church youth group had a workday to help shuffle the three Kauffman families. Mom moved from Bittinger to Grantsville; Andrews moved from Grantsville to Bittinger; and I moved from my apartment into the double-wide with Mom. I eventually adjusted to not living alone even thought I felt my concerned mom got overly alarmed sometimes. I guess that is how mothers ought to be, and I soon found out again that sometimes she was right!

Chapter 27

I had lived in my new home for only four days when Mom decided I needed to go to the doctor. The doctor was concerned about a possible IV line infection again, so they kept me in the hospital on antibiotics until the cultures came back. That way, if the results showed infection, we would be one step ahead. The first culture came back clear, so the doctor was ready to send me home. Later in the afternoon, a nurse came with a handful of supplies and a bag of antibiotics, saying, "I'm sure you are not going home today."

"Why not? They said I could go."

When the doctor came back, he told me the last culture revealed a serious fungal yeast growing in my blood. They needed to take out the infected Broviac line they had just placed with such difficulty. They then called the flight team to see if they could get a regular IV started. With my history of impossible veins, everyone was amazed when Judy found one. I was sure to remember her name—she was one valuable person to me if she could find my veins. Being stabbed for hours on end is one of my least favorite pastimes.

Mom had embroidered a twelve-animal crib quilt for each of her twenty-seven grandchildren. She credited me with the fact that she had them all complete, for the only times she worked on them were when she waited with me in doctors' offices, emergency rooms, and hospital wards. We had been in and out of the hospital so often that we were learning to know the staff members personally. One time a male nurse stuck his nose in the door saying, "I just had to stop by and see what animal you are working on this time."

When someone from social services walked in, I figured they had bad news. They did. Although the doctors were considering sending me home, they were waiting for the insurance company, which didn't want to pay for my TPN. "They say as long as you can swallow, they won't pay for it," the worker explained. "I know it's ridiculous, but they refuse to budge!"

I had been on TPN for more than ten years; now they suddenly decided they did not want to pay for it? The expense was the problem. At the hospital my "food" was costing $1,000 every twenty-four hours. After two weeks in the hospital, the supply company discharged me and needed to clear it with my insurance company before readmitting me. I couldn't imagine the headache of trying to deal with these things, and I learned to appreciate the social worker all the more. After spending most of a day on the phone, she still had not made any progress. She then talked to the doctor about our options.

Two days after finishing up the prescribed antibiotics, I felt myself getting sick. Mom asked, "What is wrong? Why are you shivering? Are you feeling all right?"

I decided to go lie down, hoping to get warmed up and find out that all was well. But a few hours later, Mom heard me groaning and could get no response from me. I felt so weak that it took all of my energy to breathe, let alone to speak. My sugar levels were fine, but I had a fever of 103.9°. I had strict orders to go back to the hospital if it went over 101.5°. They called the ambulance which took me to Grant Town where I was barely responsive for most of the night.

"Arlene, do you know where you are? What's your name?" Mom said the doctors and nurses were in and out asking questions most of the night, but I remembered little.

Very early in the morning, I roused long enough to see a male flight team nurse perched on the edge of my bed, looking as though he expected to be there a while as he tried to get enough blood for my tests. "Why didn't you use my Broviac IV line?" I asked groggily.

"I'm sorry. We can't use it until we know whether you have another infection in your line," he explained. Eventually, he found a very tiny vein in my little finger. Drip by slow drip, he finally got the blood he needed.

The doctor came in to let me know what they were doing. "Arlene, we're sending you to the Intensive Care Unit until a bed is available in the Step Down Unit, and we'll be starting you on five different antibiotics while we wait for your culture results in hopes that we'll hit the right infection if you do have one.

As the day progressed, my breathing became more labored until I was gasping for breath. My oxygen levels dropped. "I can't breathe," I gasped. I had a blood clot on my left lung, and I simply could not get adequate oxygen. When the staff worker from the respiratory unit came on the scene, he asked about my living will and whether I wanted cardio-pulmonary resuscitation or life support equipment. I had decided earlier I wanted neither, and I stuck to it. I had suffered so much in this life that I was more than willing to depart this decrepit body to go be with God.

They honored my wishes but did put a face mask with a cool mist over my face, hoping to make breathing somewhat easier. Soon the alarms went off, instantly bringing doctors and nurses swarming around me.

"Arlene, take a couple deep breaths! Can you hear me?"

"Honey, we need to move you to ICU right away. We're not equipped to give you the care you need here in the Step Down Unit. I see in your records you do not want to be put on a ventilator. Is that correct?"

"Yes. Right," I answered between gasps for breath.

"Not at all? Do you understand what that might mean?" An ICU team doctor pressured me as I desperately fought for breath.

While they were making preparations to move me to ICU, the doctor sat down beside Mom. "Mrs. Kauffman, I think we may need to put your daughter on a ventilator. Is that all right?" he asked.

"But Arlene doesn't want a ventilator or CPR. She has suffered so much and is ready to go on."

"She's so young. Do you realize what could happen if she refuses

it?" he asked Mom.

"Yes, we understand and so does Arlene. That is her choice."

It seemed to be beyond their understanding why someone so young would not want to take all measures possible in order to survive, and we were asked on different occasions if that was still my choice. In this case, I felt that I could trust my God to prolong my life or take me home according to His good purpose. We had spent enormous amounts of time and money on my body, but now we felt we needed to draw the line. Life is a precious gift, but death also can be a gift. "For to me to live is Christ, and to die is gain" (Philippians 1:21).

Chapter 28

David and Becky had come with their three children to visit me when I made a turn for the worse. It was important for Mom to have someone else with her while I was in such a serious condition. After calling the rest of the family, they then camped out in the lobby, the children making beds with the blankets and pillows the nurses provided for them.

In the meantime, I was taken back to ICU to a room which had a glass wall so that a nurse could watch over me continuously. During this time, I was 100% dependent on others for everything, including wiping my tears. I was loaded with tubes, pumps, monitors, and masks and had IV needles in my feet, arms, hands, and groin. Monitors constantly beeped, but a shrill screech from my monitor brought in a crew of nurses and doctors. They watched the screen, wondering if this would be the end.

"Arlene, can you hear me? Take a couple deep breaths for me. A couple more," until it brought relief.

Miriam and Mom were learning to read the monitors, so while they were with me, they watched them. When my oxygen level, heart rate or blood pressure dipped, they would gently encourage me: "Arlene, Arlene, take a couple deep breaths. Just a little more…" This would bring the rates up again, but only temporarily. This process exhausted me. I just felt that I would rather go to be with Jesus. Why was it taking so long? Why did my death need to stretch out like this?

The nurse then popped in the door. "Ladies, I think you need to leave. She is getting tired and needs a rest." The next time my num-

bers dipped, she insisted, "Take a deep breath, Arlene. Take a couple more."

Sunday morning, all my siblings were with me except for Alton, who was in Michigan, and dear Dad. I would so much have liked to see my father again but had no idea where we could find him.

In spite of my labored breathing, my oxygen levels continued to drop. The respiratory team kept increasing my oxygen, but to little avail. Soon they went out to the lobby to explain to the family what we were facing. They did decide to put me on a bipap, which forced moist air into my lungs through a mask. It gave me the oxygen I needed and allowed me to talk, but the bipap was only a temporary fix and could not be used for a long period of time because of its tendency to make the lungs brittle. In fact, some people cannot handle using the bipap at all. The therapist explained this to me before we used it, so I took it like a challenge, determined that with God's continued help I would give it a try.

My church was holding a week-long series of meetings. They spent time pleading with God that His will would be done in my life and that He would provide the peace and strength I needed. God answered their prayers. The saints prayed, and God gave me the strength I needed. I adjusted to the bipap and had no serious problems. They also prayed for my family in the difficult situation of making decisions that could make the difference between life and death for me. With the sorry state of my body during the best times, I knew I didn't want a ventilator.

On one of my lowest days, one of the doctors told Mom, "I'm a firm believer in letting God take us in His own time." Even though she as a doctor did what she could to save lives, she respected us for our decision. She confessed, "I think the medical world sometimes takes it too far."

Others reminded us that although the ICU doctors are trained to save the patient at all costs, we did have the right to say no to some of the more extreme measures.

Monday morning, a doctor from the Respiratory Unit came into the lobby where my family was staying. As he took Mom's hand, his tears mingled with my family's. "I'm so sorry," he said. "I'm going to be up front with you. It doesn't look good. She is entirely dependent on the oxygen we give her. I understand she does not want a ventilator, and, honestly, I think I'd make the same decision for someone in my family. But when the bipap turns off, her oxygen and heart rates drop significantly. If we remove her bipap, we are going to lose her."

My heart felt at peace. I knew that I was sheltered, safe in the arms of God. I knew that in life or death I was surrounded by His love. I was ready to move beyond this life that was now so dependent on narcotics, feeding tubes, and machines.

On one hand, I felt I was ready to take flight, ready to go with joy. At the same time I also felt a weight, like an anchor not quite allowing me to choose death. With tears streaming unchecked down my face, I asked, "Can't someone somewhere find an address or phone number for Dad? Tell him I'm dying and I want to see him. Tell him I love him and I am concerned about him."

"Arlene, we'll do our best to find him," Mom assured me. This was not the first time we had tried to reach him, but their renewed efforts did not provide any more information on Dad's whereabouts.

Barbara, a Mennonite intern sitting with somebody in the waiting room, introduced herself to us. When she found out that Mom had not been in bed for five days, she insisted that Mom come to her house for at least one full night of rest. Barbara acted as a special messenger from God to weary people in a hospital in Western Maryland. Mom found it hard to leave me for the night, but she knew how desperately she needed some rest so she could cope with the anxieties of the indefinite tomorrows.

In the morning, a doctor came in to tell me I had now developed a serious staph infection in my blood. "Do you understand this is really serious? I know you've been through a lot, but chances are that if you don't want the ventilator, it may not be long. You've had so many different infections in the past, and they seem to get worse each round." He stood by my bed and looked at me. "You still don't want the ventilator?" he asked. I shook my head. I did not want my family needing to decide when to pull the plugs. The doctor stroked my hand. "If you do pull through, it will be a miracle, but we can always hope for miracles."

"Yea, though I walk through the valley of the shadow of death, I will fear no evil, for thou art with me" (Psalm 23:4). I walked this valley of death for more than a week, and although I clearly felt God with me and often echoed the words of the song, "I am packed and ready to go," there were times when Satan tried to take away the peace I felt with God. He bombarded my mind with doubts, reminding me of mistakes I had made. During this time of standing outside the door of heaven, staring at it and wondering if maybe it would open to me in the next ten minutes, the enemy of my soul made me feel shame and doubt about actually standing before my God.

One of my brothers came in for a few minutes during the night, wiping my tears as his own rolled down his cheeks. I again felt ready to go. My whole family lived in the middle of this great struggle, hating to see me suspended in suffering, crying out for release, wanting death and wanting life. Mom writes a little about this time.

> They only allowed two family members in to see her for five to ten minutes every two hours. After days of this struggle, her suffering still had not eased, and we knew that without a miracle, she would soon be gone. One of her brothers went into the ICU with me, and at first she didn't seem to know we were in with her. My heart cried out, "O Lord, why must she suffer so? Just take her out of her misery." As we looked at her and wept, she spoke, with great difficulty.
>
> "Why is it taking so long?"
>
> "What is taking so long?" I asked gently.
>
> "Why can't I die?"
>
> I thought my heart could not break into smaller pieces.

Mom rubbed my back gently, and my brother wept as he spoke for the whole family. "We'll miss you, but don't stay here because of us. We want to be happy for you when you go." He then prayed, releasing me to God.

After ten days of waiting for a room to become available in the Family House connected to the hospital, Mom was finally notified that a room was available. This allowed her to check on me during the night without going outside.

Chapter 29

As the days progressed, to the surprise of everyone involved, I began a slow recovery. I could see the relief on the faces of those suffering with me as the intensity of the struggle eased. God had given me life for a little longer, and although in some ways I felt disappointment to be coming back to the battles of this life, I also knew that God must have more planned for me. My suffering was not yet over. I had been in ICU for nine days before they moved me back to the Step Down Unit and off of the bipap machine. I had been lying flat on my back for ten days. When the physical therapists started working with me, I could sit alone for only several minutes at a time.

After four weeks of hospital life, workers from Social Services came by to make arrangements for my release. They had predicted earlier that if I ever went home, it would only be with oxygen and a hospital bed. However, I was discharged and went home without oxygen.

Still very weak, I found that walking but a few steps made me break out in a sweat. But I could walk! I was amazed at how quickly my strength seemed to return without adequate nutrition. The insurance company was again refusing to pay the $700 daily cost for my TPN feedings, even though I was losing weight rapidly without it.

By the second day at home, I got rid of my wheelchair. A few days later I set my walker to the side. I was so excited! I knew God really was working a miracle for me, and He still had something He wanted me to do for Him. Since I could not go out to encourage people, I knew God would bring people to me. Everyone I interacted with represented a chance to build the kingdom of God. Each person who came was another reason why God still wanted me here.

I found I had many fun interactions with the Home Health Care workers who came to help me. Leanna was one who made me laugh with a story about herself. "I love to sing," she said one day when she heard the Christmas music I had playing, "but I can't carry a tune." She grinned. "So, I sing in my car where nobody can hear me. One day I was driving a state vehicle with a CB in it. After I left a patient's house, I flopped my bag on top of the CB and belted out my favorite songs, singing at the top of my voice. When I got back to the office a few hours later, there was a message waiting for me." I grinned a huge grin, and Leanna covered her face with her hands for a moment, then went on. "911 called the Home Health Care office and said that whoever was in the vehicle must be happy but is holding up the line. I wanted to drop through the floor!" We both laughed.

Nurses, X-ray technicians, Home Health Care workers, doctors— they are all people with their own stories. I do not wish illness on anyone, and I do not even wish it on myself, but being a regular patient does open up unique opportunities to communicate love and caring to others while they do their jobs.

My mother talks about this:

> Sitting in and living in the ICU waiting room brings ample opportunities to witness and minister to many people. We all have one thing in common: we are all hurting. During one of Arlene's most critical times, one man I met at the front desk was totally beside himself. His wife had a brain tumor surgery and was not doing well. He constantly paced the floor, not eating or sleeping. I had been reading the book *Comfort for the Troubled Christian*. I shared one of the thoughts with him. Later he told one of my children how much I had helped him. I have no idea what I had said, but I praise God for the chance to make a difference in someone's life.
>
> Actually, all I needed to do was look around to see someone in need of encouragement, and I know from personal experience that God is the giver of all comfort.
>
> During another one of Arlene's hospital stays, her

roommate woke me in the middle of the night asking me to come hold her hand and pray for her because she was afraid. She needed heart surgery but was not healthy enough for it; she knew she was in very critical condition. I read some verses from the Bible and prayed for her. She had never chosen to accept Jesus as her Savior, but she wanted to make that choice the night I talked with her. We both knew it was no accident that Arlene had been her roommate.

God works in mysterious ways, His wonders to perform. Wherever we are, in whatever situation we find ourselves, He can work through us if we allow Him to.

In the beginning of 2006, I had another opportunity to show my friends in the emergency room the difference that Jesus makes in our attitudes. My PICC line was leaking *again*. Of course, it was on a Friday night when we headed to Grant Town. The PICC line is generally a temporary form of intravenous access entering the vein in the upper arm and advancing toward the heart. They did not want to place the more permanent Broviac until they felt certain my infection was completely clear. The problem was that over the weekend they had no PICC line nurses. They could not replace my line.

"Maybe we can find somebody who's good with bad veins," they said. I knew that meant they would stick me in multiple places, possibly spending hours trying to find a vein. Apparently no one on duty was "good with bad veins," so I ended up waiting until Monday morning with no nourishment or intravenous medication.

"Sounds as though you had a rough weekend," the PICC line nurse said when she walked in. "It's ridiculous that they don't hire PICC line nurses seven days a week." Fifteen minutes later, after one stick and only a little pain, the PICC line was placed.

In April, I headed to the emergency room again because my J-tube broke. I could not find any home remedies that worked for long. Previously, when it came out I had sometimes been able to push it back in. I had even used soda to open the tube when it was clogged!

This time, I had tried crazy glue, but it did not hold. The ER doctor ordered a CT scan because of the unhealthy-looking discharge at the tube site. Because of my enlarged stomach and discomfort, he called the surgeon in. They feared I had another blocked bowel.

"Listen to my plan," I told the surgeon, Dr. Jackson. "If you give me a couple of tubes to take along home, I can replace them myself when they need replacing. Then I won't need to drive so far and you won't need to do it. Sound like a deal?"

He grinned. "Maybe you could, but that would defeat the whole purpose if we didn't have the pleasure of seeing you. We like your smile."

Dr. Jackson often looked stern as he peered over the spectacles sitting on his nose. When I first met him, he had not cracked a smile. However, I soon found an interesting personality underneath that mask. I had fun getting him to smile, and I discovered that he could even be a bit mischievous!

He went on, "Seriously, though, changing these tubes is really a job for surgeons. Even the nurses don't do it. I'm not sure how smart it is for you to slip the tubes back in place, even though so far it has seemed to work for you. You just might be better than some of us. I know you and your mom are definitely acquiring some nursing skills! Our main concern would be that they are where they belong."

He put in a larger tube, hoping that it would stay. We left, but had not gone very far before we turned around and came back because of the irritation and pain of the larger tube. They went back to the original size and hoped for the best.

Chapter 30

By June, it had been six months since I had stopped taking TPN because of the problem of paying for it. I had lost 44 pounds and continued losing strength. "We should see if we can get you on enough tube feedings through the J-tube," one doctor suggested. "Maybe we can do without the TPN. It raises the potential for line infections and blood clots, and it is also hard on the liver," one doctor on the team suggested. Another spoke up, "It looks like you're literally starving to death in front of our eyes. Your blood work shows you're not getting enough nutrition from the little food you eat and from the tube feedings. Everyone on the team agreed they needed to change something. They needed to get me back on the TPN, but I knew there was no way we could pay for it.

In early July I lost my balance and fell for the third time. I needed to crawl to a small stand so I could pull myself up, but it took extreme effort. Martha, who was in the house and heard some commotion, came to investigate. "Arlene, what's wrong?"

This was not the first time I had tripped over my own feet. She noticed that I tended to drag my left leg and my face also drooped a bit on the same side. A little puffiness even appeared around my left eye. I called the doctor, and he agreed it had probably been a mini-stroke. He ordered more blood work and a CT scan of my head. The CT scan showed no serious damage that might have resulted from a stroke. "At least you know now you have a brain," a nurse grinned. "Some of the rest of us aren't sure if we do."

A doctor teased, "You're just making us work harder for a diagnosis of your imbalance!" Others felt the weakness resulted from malnutrition. They did determine, however, that part of the problem was Drop Foot Syndrome, a weakness in the muscles that flex the ankle and toes, a possible result of diabetes, injury to the dorsiflexor muscles, or a stroke. The doctors ordered more tests, none of which I enjoyed.

In the first test, they sent electrical shocks through my legs to measure the muscle impulses. They found delayed impulses in numerous places. For the second test, they came with a two-inch needle, sticking it straight into the muscles of my feet and legs, one after the other, each stick less than a minute apart until I thought I had had enough for one day. It got a little hard on my nerves, though I thought my nerves had held up rather well all these years.

There were two nurses and two doctors watching the screen as they pricked. Another doctor, who never looked at me, wanted his turn with the needle. He went straight in with the needle, repeatedly, yet never looked at me. I tried hard to strike up a conversation, or at least to get him to recognize that I had feelings. This guy had come in, interested only in the screen and not at all in me as a person. After an hour and a half, he did manage a smile and there was actually brief eye contact.

But there was good news with the bad. The Social Services worker nearly bounded into the room, all excited. "Arlene! Your insurance cleared the TPN! We can use it!"

Chapter 31

After numerous hospitalizations because of blocked bowels, we felt no closer to any long-term solutions. My belly had swollen so much that it looked like I was eight months pregnant. Finally the doctor admitted that he saw only one thing to try: a colostomy. He wanted to remove my colon, now grossly oversized and paralyzed.

For weeks, I tossed and turned with indecision. "Never go through major surgery without your family's full support; don't rush your answer," a nurse had said. I knew this was good advice. But how could we know what the best choice would be? If we did nothing, the misery was guaranteed to continue. Yet surgery was dangerous and dreaded. I was afraid the stoma (opening for excrement) would smell. I also wondered if I had not gone through enough of this sort of unpleasant ordeals. My friends and family joined me in asking God for peace as we made this decision. Although not all my qualms were satisfied, God did answer my prayer, and we scheduled surgery for July 6, 2007.

The week prior to the surgery, I attended a huge reunion that brought together my father's large extended family. All ninety of my cousins, uncles, and aunts spent time praying for me that day. While they and many others prayed, I felt so cared for. I knew God had once again used other people to show me His love. The worry I had felt about this serious surgery shrank under the peace I felt as I relaxed, calmed not only in my emotions but also in my heart. Surrounded by people who cared, I felt ready for what I knew from past experiences would be an excruciatingly difficult experience.

The hospital admitted me two days before my surgery so they could get my blood consistency regulated and stabilized before surgery. I regularly took blood thinner because of two previous blood clots. The doctors knew that every complication that could appear likely would. My ill-fated body had little going for it.

The surgical team removed the entire colon through an incision from the breast bone to the pelvic bone. During the surgery, they also removed a hernia from an earlier surgery site and changed the J-tube I had had for twelve years. They also moved it to the left side of my belly so they could use the right side for the dreaded stoma. I kept the Broviac IV line which, connected to the heart, continued supplying those all-important medications to my blood.

Sometime after surgery, the stoma nurse stopped by to check on the stoma where my small intestine protruded about an inch out through the opening. "It's the most beautiful stoma ever," she grinned. "You should be proud of your juicy red strawberry."

"Let's call it what it is," I thought, "a stoma." I still felt somewhat disgusted by all that my body endured, but after six weeks of little trouble or mess, I admitted it might not be quite as bad as I had expected.

Another kind of battle continued inside me. I knew people said they cared, and certainly many of them did, but Arlene and her serious surgeries were becoming old hat. How often had I been in the hospital with complications and severe pain? The previous experiences did nothing to lessen the pain, the worry, and the loneliness now. There were days when no visitors came, no cards arrived, no flowers were sent. Had they forgotten? Were they thinking, *It's just Arlene. She's in the hospital again?* I could not allow myself to cave under these heavy thoughts. "Lo, I am with you alway" (Matthew 28:20), Someone has said. And that Someone never lies.

I know my family suffered with me on the days of painful existence after surgery. Mom stayed at the hospital's Family House, and my sisters and sisters-in-law took turns relieving her so that she could relax and catch up at home. They turned me in bed, helped me sit up, supported me on my short walks, and prayed that the nurses would stay away during my brief naps between doses of morphine. I

needed a lot of help during those first weeks of severe pain. My family provided a lot of physical, emotional, and spiritual support.

One day while Miriam stayed with me, Wes brought their children in to see me. When four-year-old Jonathan spied me, he came running with shining eyes, jumping up and down and laughing; he could hardly contain his excitement! I sat in a chair while little Angelina tucked the corners of the blanket up around my neck, patting me and asking, "Does that feel good?" Of course it felt good if it was Angelina who did it!

When Miriam came into my room after seeing her family leave, she smiled and told me that Jonathan said, "I am worried about Arlene." Both of the children, along with my other nieces and nephews, pray for me regularly. Their genuine love and concern has brought such joy to me. They have been some of the most precious gifts God has given me.

As I walked through the halls on my short walks, and as I viewed the world through the doors of my hospital room, I wondered if the hospital is not a place where people have unwell spirits as well as bodies. I wondered if staff members need healing as well as the patients. I wondered if sometimes patients bring healing to the staff. I knew that this is what I wanted to do. While they helped me take care of my sickly body, I looked for ways to help them care for their souls.

On one particularly busy day, one of my favorite nurses asked, "Can I hide myself here in your room?" She grinned and said, "I need some peace while I do my paperwork!" I really do want people to sense the presence of God in my room, and I always smile with delight when I hear nurses during the shift change discussing who cares for which patient and saying, "No, I want Arlene."

Chapter 32

Now, after many years of physical suffering, I wonder how I can keep up the fight much longer. We are becoming practiced in the rituals of hospitalization, surgeries, placing tubes, carrying pumps, and injecting medication for chronic, painful illness. We have been through all of this many times. I continue with chronic pancreatitis pain even though I do use $700 worth of morphine each month, injecting it into my Broviac every four hours, and I am also taking Phenergan for nausea. I still take tube feedings through the J-tube day and night while the waste empties itself into a bag at my side. Wherever I go, my pumps go also.

I understand that this chronic illness with pain and nausea will be a part of me for the rest of my life, for even if the medical world reaches another level of breakthrough and discovery, it cannot reverse what has been done in previous surgeries. My goal now is to complete this journey of life as a living testimony to those with whom I come in contact, especially to anyone else who is hurting, be it someone in the doctor's office, in the hospital, or perhaps those who learn to know me in this book, both patients and caregivers.

People observe how we cope, and they are looking for a place to go for help. We who have found that place have the responsibility to show others. God's Word is rich with promises, not for an easy life, but a promise of His presence.

> When you pass through the waters,
> I will be with you;
> and when you pass through the rivers,
> they will not sweep over you.

When you walk through the fire,
you will not be burned;
the flames will not set you ablaze.
For I am the LORD, your God,
the Holy One of Israel, your Savior
(Isaiah 43:2, 3, NIV).

I need to remind myself periodically that if He takes something away from me, He will give me something better. It may mean trading my life here on earth for a home in heaven. It may mean trading health for a deeper faith and a unique ministry in suffering. My experiences of fear and pain and distress all have one word stamped over them: *temporary*. I long for the day when God lifts me out of this sin-ravaged campground and gives me a new tent. Then my reality will instead be defined by the word *eternal*. "For the things which are seen are temporal; but the things which are not seen are eternal" (2 Corinthians 4:18).

One day, God will open my eyes, and I will see clearly what I now see through clouds of pain. On the last page of the last chapter of my story, He will stamp *The End,* and that will be only the beginning of a brand new story, each page better than the last. I know this, for His love and His mercy endure forever.

Epilogue

On December 27, 2007, Arlene closed one book and began another. After more than thirty years of doctors' appointments, hospitals, vague diagnoses, and pain medication, Arlene left her body, her tattered tent, behind. The body that was buried lacked a thyroid, a gall bladder, a pancreas, and a colon. It had been poked and prodded, tested and tortured for many years, but the spirit that left was intact and joined the God Arlene served all her life.

Although the colostomy in July improved the tight, miserable feeling she had so long experienced, Arlene often said, "I just don't feel good." Between August and December, she lost thirty pounds and was admitted to the hospital three times.

Two weeks before her death, her mother, Matilda, brought her home from the hospital on a Friday evening. "I'm afraid we'll do you more harm than good if we keep you here," the doctor had told Arlene. That was the last drive home from the hospital that Matilda and Arlene would ever make together. The next morning, Arlene told her mother, "I think I'm on my way home." For once, she had made doctor appointments she will never have to keep. She had another appointment: one she had been wishing for and anticipating for years.

Shaky, uncoordinated, and still dealing with the never-ending pain, Arlene continued losing weight, but she did not want to eat. Soon she could not eat but vomited up everything. Her digestive system simply would not work, and even her much-needed thyroid pills would not stay down. Matilda tried crushing the pills and feeding them in one spoonful of applesauce or through her J-tube, but to

no avail. These days were miserable for Arlene, and on December 19, hospice came and assisted the family in making the last days as bearable as possible. Family members stayed with her around the clock, sometimes talking and sometimes just holding her hand or rubbing her arm to let her know that they were walking with her through this Valley of the Shadow of Death.

Arlene slept a lot the last week, and sleep was a blessed relief from her physical misery. By Christmas Day, she had reached a plateau of sorts. Her sleep seemed coma-like, and when she woke, it was usually brief. When her oldest brother Alton and his family arrived from out of state, Arlene recognized and spoke to each of her nieces and nephews. "I thought maybe I would be gone before you got here," she told Alton. Her nieces and nephews always brought Arlene great delight, and Matilda tells of one day when Regina, Arlene's sister-in-law, walked in with eight-month-old Bronson. Arlene's eyes lit up, and she smiled, managing to wave a little. He returned the wave, and ten minutes later when she drifted off to sleep, she was still smiling.

On that last Christmas Day, some of her nieces and nephews were a few miles away at a Christmas gathering with their mother's side of the family. When they got news that Arlene was awake, they and their cousins stacked and double-stacked themselves into three vehicles and went to sing Christmas carols on Arlene's porch. Arlene looked out the window and smiled, even waving weakly as they left. Her voice had become so weak that it was difficult to understand her, but when they had all gone, she said, "That made me so tired." This was Arlene's last sentence.

It was close to midnight on December 26 when Arlene's breathing changed and her immediate family gathered around her bed. She probably did not hear them, but as a final testament to her life, they recited the twenty-third Psalm, and her brother David took her hand and prayed, giving her back to the One who had created her for His glory. Soon her breathing slowed, and at 2:41 a.m., it stopped.

According to *The American Heritage College Dictionary,* an epilogue is "a short section at the end of a literary…work, often discussing the future of its characters." Arlene's future has not been cut short; it has only begun. While we know little of that future, and any discussion of it would be woefully inadequate, we can all look forward to sharing that one final glorious epilogue with her and with the God whose love sustains us all.

* * * * * * * * * * * *

The story Arlene tells here is the honest yearning of her heart. Although her longing to go home to Jesus was real and that wish finally was granted, one of her deepest longings never was fulfilled: she died without having told her daddy goodbye. Arlene lets us see her doubts, her loneliness, and her failings. She persuades us she is human, but we know she was an extraordinary human because of her God's extraordinary grace. God is "Stronger than Pain."

Arlene's mother knew her better than anyone else, and her stories show that Arlene's true desire was to live for her Maker. Matilda writes, "The worse [Arlene] hurt, the busier she made herself. She made many beautiful cards to sell. She spent hours and hours on that, often far into the night. 'I can't sit and pity myself,' she'd say."

Even in pain, Arlene somehow radiated an exuberance that almost makes one think that Pollyanna's impossible optimism deserves more credit than many people give it. The story of her "gladness" is astonishing. Sit on one end to squash her happiness and her smiling face pops up on the other. As Matilda says, "I didn't know how she could keep her hopes so high; she was always cheerfully looking forward to better days."

With others who knew her, I [Lori Yoder] can testify to Arlene's genuine desire to show other people the difference that God can make in a person's life, even when that life is full of physical pain and unfulfilled hopes. I think now of one particular incident, amusing because of its absurdity.

After getting the results from her routine blood work, the pain clinic called to set up an appointment with Arlene. The doctor walked into the office, and with no ado whatsoever, declared that

they needed to wean Arlene off her morphine since it was dangerous to use morphine and alcohol at the same time. Completely taken aback, Arlene insisted that she had *not* started drinking as a way of dealing with her troubles. Her wildly fluctuating sugar problems along with all the medication she was taking must have caused the false report. The doctor refused to agree to talk to family members for verification although Arlene continued to insist that she never drank alcoholic beverages. He sent her to make an appointment to see a psychiatrist for her depression and drug addiction.

With her characteristic spontaneity, Arlene asked me vehemently, "Now, isn't that ridiculous?" The idea of Arlene drowning her troubles in liquor was truly ludicrous. Arlene saw the humor in it, but was still appalled that anyone would think that God had not been big enough, good enough, or strong enough to see her through her pain, and that depression had driven her to alcohol.

Arlene visited the psychiatrist and the situation was eventually cleared up, but Matilda tells me this incident really agitated Arlene. The great purpose of her life was to showcase God's grace, and she worried that this might in some way bring disgrace to God. Many of us wonder how anyone can endure what Arlene endured, but Arlene knew how: it was God's amazing grace.

I was part of the group that sang Christmas carols outside Arlene's window on Christmas Day, less than two days before she died. Weak as she was, when she saw me, she smiled, and her eyes smiled, and she lifted her hand for a moment. Arlene lived with more physical pain than anyone I have ever known, but she had made up her mind years before that she would keep hoping, keep seeing the goodness in the world, and keep thanking God for all His good gifts.

Yes, God's grace is "Stronger Than Pain."

Order Form

To order, send this completed order form to:
Vision Publishers
P.O. Box 190
Harrisonburg, VA 22803
Fax: 540-437-1969
E-mail: orders@vision-publishers.com
www.vision-publishers.com

_____   _____
Name   Date

_____   _____
Mailing Address   Phone

_____
City   State   Zip

Stronger Than Pain   Qty. _____ x $8.99 each = _____
              (Please call for quantity discounts - 877/488-0901)

Price _____

Virginia residents add 5% sales tax _____

Ohio residents add applicable sales tax _____

Shipping & handling __$3.90___

Grand Total _____

All Payments in US Dollars

❏ Check #_____

❏ Money Order   ❏ Visa

❏ MasterCard   ❏ Discover

Persons Name on Card _____

Card # __|__|__|__| __|__|__|__| __|__|__|__| __|__|__|__|

3-digit code from signature panel __|__|__| Exp. Date __|__|__|__|

Thank you for your order!
For a complete listing of our books write for our catalog.
Bookstore inquiries welcome

Order Form

To order, send this completed order form to:
Vision Publishers
P.O. Box 190
Harrisonburg, VA 22803
Fax: 540-437-1969
E-mail: orders@vision-publishers.com
www.vision-publishers.com

_____   _____
Name   Date

_____   _____
Mailing Address   Phone

_____
City   State   Zip

Stronger Than Pain   Qty. _____ x $8.99 each = _____
(Please call for quantity discounts - 877/488-0901)

Price _____

Virginia residents add 5% sales tax _____

Ohio residents add applicable sales tax _____

Shipping & handling ___$3.90_____

Grand Total _____

All Payments in US Dollars

❒ Check #_____

❒ Money Order   ❒ Visa

❒ MasterCard   ❒ Discover

Persons Name on Card _____

Card # __|__|__|__| __|__|__|__| __|__|__|__| __|__|__|__|

3-digit code from signature panel __|__|__| Exp. Date __|__|__|__|

Thank you for your order!
For a complete listing of our books write for our catalog.
Bookstore inquiries welcome